A New Agenda for Education

edited by
Eileen M. Gardner

The Heritage Foundation

Library of Congress Catalog Card Number 84-63078
ISBN 0-89195-037-0
Copyright © 1985 by The Heritage Foundation

Table of Contents

Foreword   v

Introduction   vii

Chapter 1   1
The Demise of the Teaching Profession
by Annette Kirk and Russell Kirk

Chapter 2   13
Public and Private Schools
by K. Alan Snyder

Chapter 3   27
The Growth of the Federal Role in Education
by Eileen M. Gardner

Chapter 4   47
Higher Education Today
by Philip F. Lawler

Chapter 5   59
The Courts and Education
by Thomas R. Ascik

Chapter 6   79
A New Agenda for Education

Contributors   85

Foreword—The Conservative Agenda

To state that the United States is becoming increasingly conservative and is re-embracing traditional values today barely elicits a protest, even from the most dedicated leftist. Few can ignore the message of the 1984 election, which followed the impressive conservative gains of 1978 and the sweep of 1980. Public opinion polls, election results and volumes of anecdotal evidence demonstrate that Americans have turned to conservatives for answers to the most important problems facing the U.S.

In a number of areas, conservative answers are well known and well formulated. This surely is the case regarding government regulation of the economy, the disincentives created by high taxes and the need for a strong national defense. In other areas of pressing national concern, however, the conservative approach is not so well developed. Very often, to be sure, conservative analysts have mounted a powerful critique of the liberal approach to a problem. There are, for instance, strong and persuasive conservative cases made against liberal programs for the poor or civil rights or education. Less often, however, have conservatives described how they would replace discredited liberal concepts and programs with specific measures that would help build an opportunity society. While the conservative critique, therefore, is well known, the conservative agenda is not.

It is to encourage evolution of such agendas that The Heritage Foundation inaugurates a new series of *Critical Issues* publications. Inviting the participation of some of the conservative community's most creative and innovative thinkers, each *Critical Issue* will examine a particular problem and attempt to go beyond critique to suggesting an agenda for action. Upcoming *Critical Issues* will propose a conservative agenda for welfare, U.S. relations with the Soviet Union, civil rights and help for underdeveloped countries. With this volume, *A New Agenda for Education,* The Heritage Foundation is pleased to launch the new series.

> Burton Yale Pines
> Vice President
> Director of Research

Introduction

Through almost all of U.S. history, local control of education has been a hallmark of American society. The neighborhood school, the thousands of popularly elected school boards, and the county and state education agencies all contributed to one of America's major achievements—free and universal education. This educational "system" produced the inventors, scientists, engineers, philosophers, businessmen, labor leaders, teachers, and politicians who made the U.S. the envy of the world. Yet about a quarter century ago, local control of education came under unrelenting attack. Gradually neighborhood schools were consolidated into larger units with the promised benefits of expanded and more efficient education programs. Promises of improved efficiency, equity, and quality also brought the executive, legislative, and judicial branches of the federal government into local education. As a result, America's traditional local education system began to give way to growing centralization. At the same time, an ever decreasing portion of the students' school day was devoted to the primary function of education: academic learning.

Centralization in American education gained considerable strength from the U.S. Supreme Court's 1954 decision, *Brown v. Board of Education,* which mandated desegregation in the nation's schools. And the impetus accelerated when the nation became alarmed by the educational implications of the 1957 launching of the Soviet space satellite Sputnik I. With the Elementary and Secondary Education Act of 1965, the federal presence in education was on its way to becoming federal control.

Spurring centralization was the move to use the schools as instruments of social policy. This was justified by four questionable assumptions:

1. Since man's nature supposedly is determined by society and the environment in which he lives, inequality of result is evidence of discrimination.

2. The "state" has the duty to rectify such inequalities of result.

3. Centralization is the best way to improve education because localities have proved incapable of helping special populations.

4. More money will improve education.

These assumptions became dogma. They are rooted in modern man's denial of a higher power and in his refusal to acknowledge that it is internal man who shapes his external condition, and not the other way around.

The experience of the past quarter century refutes the four assumptions. Billions of dollars have been spent on special compensatory programs, which have not accomplished their goals; indeed, some spending has even made the situation worse. For example, as education expenditures have gone up, there has been a dramatic drop in academic achievement, morals, responsible citizenship, and even basic work skills. Centralization in education, moreover, has restricted the able and reduced all to the equality of the lowest common denominator. Any criticism of this is silenced as "elitist." Yet even a cursory examination reveals techniques that constrain, fragment, and eventually will destroy American education. Among these:

- There is an unrelenting attempt to sever cause from effect. Any effort to link the two is dismissed as simplistic. For example, the National Education Association has rejected testing teachers on their knowledge of academic subject matter as an irrelevant measure of teaching competence. Yet, more than any other factor, a lack of subject matter knowledge (the cause) guarantees poor teaching (the effect).

- Remedial programs with large bureaucracies are lavishly funded to tackle problems the bureaucracies themselves have created. It is estimated, for example, that 50 to 75 percent of the children labeled "learning disabled" are mislabeled. Many of these mislabeled children are pulled from a coherent program of regular classroom instruction to be "remediated" in a resource room that often lacks instructional viability and coordination with the existing education curriculum. Cadres of special needs personnel and accompanying administrative bureaucracies are then installed to serve these newly found "special needs" students.

- The unattainable ideal of manifest equality has been converted into a "right." Resources are expended to guarantee this, thereby usurping the proper mission, and weakening the institutions, of education. In the 1970s, for example, responding to affirmative action policies, universities established special recruiting drives, admissions standards, and remedial courses for minorities. According to the 1983 National Commission on Excellence in Education report, "Between 1975 and 1980, remedial mathematics courses in public 4-year colleges increased by 72 percent and now constitute one-quarter of all mathematics courses taught in those institutions."* Further, many of these colleges assigned full college credit to these remedial courses. As a result, no longer is a college degree automatic testament to high intellectual attainment.

- Data that disprove the dogma often are disregarded, manipulated, or suppressed.

- There is a campaign to separate man from his source—God. Prayer has been removed from the schools, and in *Epperson v.*

---

*A Nation At Risk, A Report by the National Commission on Excellence in Education. Available from the Superintendent of Documents, U.S. Government Printing Office, Washington, D.C., 20402.

Arkansas (1968) even religious motives for educational policy were impugned.

Thus has centralization failed American education. It has corrupted the education process and undermined the primary missions of the schools—the acquisition of academic skills, the development of a responsible citizenry, and the search for truth. Direct regulation, categorical grants, and court decisions have influenced admissions, faculty appointments, curricula, classroom procedures, research, internal governance—mainly to the detriment of the education process. Time, energy, and resources have been diverted from educating and channeled into paperwork, meetings, and other government-imposed requirements.

An ominous offshoot of this increased centralization has been the use of the federal bureaucracy as a base from which powerful and unaccountable special interest groups have operated. The loss of local control of schools to those groups has eroded the flexibility needed to respond to local situations. Local educators now find themselves hamstrung by mandates and regulations that operate to the detriment of their schools.

Reversing this trend in U.S. education calls for significant policy changes. The essays and action agenda in this volume detail the steps to be taken. They are:

1. Removing or substantially reducing Washington's role in education. The federal court decisions that have changed the purpose of American education must be reversed. The federal mandates that have diluted curricula by catering to special interests at the expense of the welfare of the whole must be cancelled. And the targeted federal monies that have lured education from its traditional path onto byways charted by special interest groups must be rescinded and then reallocated not for specific purposes but for general purpose block grants to the states.

The federal role in education should be to define and encourage excellence, making available the most up-to-date and well-proved methods for its attainment and rewarding people and programs that exemplify excellence in education. This the Reagan Administration has done through the Secondary School Recognition Program and the President's Academic Fitness Awards Program, for example.

To diminish the federal role in education is to restore control to the states and localities. This was the widespread view of those secondary school principals honored in 1983 by the U.S. Department of Education for excellence in education. Of the 152 honored, 63 responded to a Heritage Foundation survey which asked them to explain their success. Typical of the responses was that of Principal James Carlile of Sunset High School in Beaverton, Oregon: "I believe the most important factor in success at the local school level is a reasonable amount of autonomy with respect to staffing, program design, and expenditure of money."

2. Restoring to education its primary function—the academic and moral training of the nation's youth. At the very least, quotas, often seen as having replaced the emphasis on quality education, should be deleted from affirmative action programs, and education institutions should be freed of government interference unless a specific, concrete charge of illegal discrimination has been filed. This would allow educational institutions to focus on academic goals. In addition, court-ordered busing, which has resegregated the nation's schools through "white flight," should be terminated and replaced with voluntary programs of integration when racial discrimination in educational opportunities is judged to have occurred.

3. Revising teacher training so that capable people who can master the science and the art of teaching will be attracted into the classroom. It is usually assumed (by the National Education Association, for example) that this can be accomplished best by offering higher salaries. Yet higher salaries, unconnected with merit incentives, tend to attract those interested mainly in making money rather than in imparting knowledge. When higher salaries are paid, they must reward merit and achievement. Teaching certification should be contingent upon rigorous testing of knowledge in subject matter, and not merely upon knowledge of teaching methods and techniques. New Jersey's alternate route to teaching certification is a model that other states should examine. Programs such as the one at the Harvard Graduate School of Education, which trains corporate retirees to become teachers of mathematics and science, show promise and warrant close scrutiny.

4. Allowing competition in education. The current near monopoly of the public schools, buttressed by the power of the teachers' unions, provides little incentive within the education establishment for ways to improve education. Education must be opened to competition through a system of tuition tax credits and vouchers. In this way effective education programs can clearly stand out from ineffective ones. The success of such programs, which would have to meet the exacting demands of parents, would spur other programs to emulation and would drive out those that are ineffective.

Centralization leads to centralized control, and centralized control works poorly in the domain of education. Indeed, education is not even mentioned in the U.S. Constitution. Undoubtedly this is because our Founding Fathers understood what modern America has had to learn the hard way: Education is essentially a state, local, and parental matter. The closer education is to those it affects, the better education works. Let this, then, be the lesson, and let the U.S. move now to make the necessary changes to avoid having to learn it again.

1

The Demise of the Teaching Profession

by
Annette Kirk and Russell Kirk

A fair number of able teachers survive in the American apparatus of public instruction. But for most teachers, the term "mediocre" must suffice; and some ought never to be permitted to enter a classroom. Consider the remarks of Dr. Terrel H. Bell, former Secretary of Education, at a recent Washington conference of educational officials from fifteen countries. "The condition of the teaching profession is at an all-time low," Bell declared. "We're getting tomorrow's teachers from the bottom of the spectrum of human ability."[1]

Even if there is some hyperbole in the Secretary's lament, a sober series of studies by Phillip C. Schlechty and Victor S. Vance, summarized in the *Phi Delta Kappan,* reveals a marked decline of ability among people entering the teaching profession. In a paper prepared for the National Institute of Education, "Institutional Responses to the Quality/Quantity Issue in Teacher Training," Schlechty and Vance begin by pointing out "that there has been a substantial decline in recent years in the absolute number and proportion of college graduates preparing to teach, and that those who are preparing to teach and those who enter teaching score less well on measures of academic ability than did teacher education majors and practicing teachers in the not so distant past."[2]

The general public—especially parents with children enrolled in the public schools—has become distressed at the indifference or incompetence of many teachers; and in consequence, many state legislatures have begun to discuss reforms; some legislatures already have acted. Even the U.S. Congress has declared its displeasure with the present state of "teacher recruitment, selection, training, certification, competency, and licensing." In a Joint Resolution in early 1984, Congress recommended that the states establish commissions to look into such

---

[1] Terrel H. Bell, addressing conference on Quality in Education at American Enterprise Institute, Washington, quoted by Thomas Toch, "Nations Share Education Concerns," *Education Week,* May 9, 1984.
[2] Philip S. Schlechty and Victor S. Vance, "Institutional Responses to the Quality/Quantity Issue in Teacher Training," *Phi Delta Kappan,* October 1983, p. 94.

concerns, with particular attention to the report of the National Commission on Excellence in Education.

That report, *A Nation at Risk* (April 1983) contains stern criticisms of the present sunken state of the teaching profession: "The Commission found that not enough of the academically able students are being attracted to teaching; that teacher preparation programs need substantial improvement; that the professional working life of teachers is on the whole unacceptable; and that a serious shortage of teachers exists in key fields." Among the particulars:

> Too many teachers are being drawn from the bottom quarter of graduating high school and college students.
>
> The teacher preparation curriculum is weighted heavily with courses in "educational methods" at the expense of courses in subjects to be taught. A survey of 1,350 institutions training teachers indicated that 41 percent of the time of elementary school teacher candidates is spent in education courses, which reduces the amount of time available for subject matter courses....
>
> Half of the newly employed mathematics, science, and English teachers are not qualified to teach these subjects; fewer than one-third of U.S. high schools offer physics taught by qualified teachers.[3]

This dismay has spread to the American Federation of Teachers. Albert Shanker, that union's president, in 1984 told the Senate Committee on Labor and Human Resources: "If we don't require an examination for new teachers, we are not serious about fighting declining standards. Teaching cannot afford to recruit from people who rank at the bottom among college graduates."[4]

The Problem

The lack of talents and of preparation among American teachers is not the only reason why American schooling (the most costly in the world) does too little for mind and character; but it is one important reason. Why does the U.S. not have better teachers? Among the reasons: Dreary teacher training; the melancholy consequences of teacher tenure; teachers' unions: what they are and what they might be; and diversion of schooling focus.

Dreary Teacher Training

A major cause of this deficiency is the boring and anti-intellectual character of most programs for training teachers. Schools and depart-

---

[3]*A Nation at Risk* (U.S. Department of Education, 1983), pp. 22-23.
[4]Albert Shanker, quoted by Cindy Currence in "Educators Urge New Approaches," *Education Week*, November 16, 1983.

ments of Education (once called pedagogy), with a few honorable exceptions, are centers of tenured dullness, held in low esteem by professors in academic departments, and still more unpopular with intelligent undergraduates. In many universities and colleges, surveys have shown that Education majors rank lower in intelligence and aptitude tests than do majors in any other field; also they receive lower grades in college than do any other body of students (this despite the fact that "grade inflation" long has been worse in departments of Education than in other disciplines).[5] When those Education majors graduate, they remain lowest in grade averages and test scores. Why?

Because the dreary emphasis of nearly all courses in pedagogy repels able young people, they turn to disciplines offering more challenge to reason and imagination. A few earnest young men and women, bent upon teaching as a vocation, persist in teacher preparation, enduring a dismal Education curriculum, gritting their teeth; although deprived of much subject matter knowledge by the requirement that many of their limited credit-hours must be wasted upon Education, some of these devoted souls fight their way over pedagogical obstacles to become good teachers eventually. But these are a small minority of the persons certified as teachers. The doctrinaire incompetence of schools and departments of Education succeeds in deterring most able undergraduates from entering the teaching profession—as if professors of Education were bent upon perpetuating the witticism, "Those who can, do; those who can't, teach; those who can't teach, teach teachers."

There exists virtually no avenue of escape from this. For state departments of public instruction require that public school teachers (and in many states, teachers in independent schools also) be certified by state authorities. To be certified, they must have completed sufficient courses in methods and approaches, the number of courses varying from state to state.

The colleges, schools, and departments of Education, in turn, tend to be dominated by the American Association of Colleges for Teacher Education (AACTE), in which there has persisted the ideology of John Dewey, William Heard Kilpatrick, George S. Counts, and other "instrumentalists" and "social adjustment" doctrinaires of yesteryear. Moreover, universities and colleges that train teachers get into difficulty if they are not accredited by the National Council for the Accreditation of Teacher Education (NCATE), which previously has resisted any reforms of teacher training. In short, a kind of interlocking directorate—whose prejudices and methods are those that prevailed at Teachers College, Columbia, in former days—effectually

---

[5]The *New York Times,* August 28, 1983.

have controlled the educating of the nation's teachers. They have been allied with the National Education Association, which throughout its various metamorphoses has set its face against any restoration of learning.

Thus scholars in the humane and scientific disciplines virtually have been excluded from influence upon the training of teachers. Most candidates for teaching posts have been schooled as if they were enrolled in the "normal schools" and "normal colleges" of yore—those institutions originally intended to convert high school graduates into teachers by exposing them to a year or two of courses in pedagogy. From those normal schools, indeed, most departments of Education are directly descended; many state colleges and universities are swollen outgrowths of normal schools and teachers' colleges.

The dominant theme of teacher training is "how to teach." In consequence, the more credits in Education accumulated by a prospective teacher, the less prepared that student is for teaching any subject matter discipline; and the more his abilities have been blunted by the boredom of the typical Education curriculum. To be certified as a teacher, a candidate must plod through a system that reduces his effective preparation for real teaching. Thus the most significant single factor in the decline of the attractiveness of teaching appears to have been the alliance of dreary Education curricula with a system of certification calculated to eliminate the fit.

Able young people have difficulty, then, in entering at all upon the vocation of teaching. But suppose a qualified college graduate does succeed in running the Education gauntlet and obtains certification: what then? The aspiring new teacher enters a realm in which ability is discouraged.

The Melancholy Consequences of Teacher Tenure

In no other occupation is mediocrity—or positive incompetence—so thoroughly entrenched as in the teaching profession today. In the learned professions, strict entrance examinations are required; competition tends to weed out the inferior practitioners; and means exist for disqualifying physicians, lawyers, accountants, and other professionals who engage in malpractice. In commerce and industry, the necessity for maintaining a balance sheet is a powerful motive for dismissing the incompetent or the indolent. But teachers, once certified and employed, may be almost impossible to remove, no matter how badly they teach. They are sheltered by tenure statutes, enacted in recent years in many states.

Originally tenure was confined to universities and colleges—where a case, if rather an uneasy one, may be made for permanent tenure of posts. But the case for tenure for school teachers is shaky. Few teachers have gone through the exacting intellectual discipline required of professors holding doctorates; and university tenure is granted only after a lengthy probation and due deliberation by peer committees and university administrators; also reasons exist why professors in higher education (concerned often with matters of speculation) may require protections unwarranted for school teachers (concerned principally with imparting a body of received information).

Presumably the concept behind teacher tenure is the idea that teachers ought to be guaranteed lifelong employment, regardless of what political and moral doctrines they may entertain and teach. But are they engaged to thrust their own opinions, however eccentric, upon boys and girls—regardless of what the community wishes to have taught to the rising generation? And why should teachers be so privileged, when clergymen, salespersons, civil servants, factory workers, and everybody else are not so protected by statute?

Whatever may be said of the theory of tenure, the practical consequences of that privilege have been baneful for the public schools. In many districts, tenure becomes automatic after a relatively short term of employment, with no examinations and little assessment of performance. Thereafter it becomes extremely difficult for administrators or school boards to remove any teacher. Discharged teachers may turn to litigation and obtain reinstatement or extract heavy damages. It is far easier for adminstrators to sigh, shrug—and leave incompetent, indolent, insolent, or malign teachers in charge of classrooms. The principal sufferers are the students, there by compulsion—and the better teachers, who thus bear a burden proportionately heavier.

"Deadwood" teachers awake contempt among pupils for the teaching profession, the school, and learning itself. The toleration of such incompetence disheartens the abler teachers, many of whom therefore seek and find greener pastures in occupations that reward integrity and ability rather than indifference and mediocrity. "She was a good teacher, as good teachers go; and as good teachers go, she went."

No real improvement of public instruction can occur until the incompetent practitioners of teaching are weeded out. This will require drastic alteration in tenure statutes and practices.

To be sure, a major reason why teacher tenure obtained general adoption was the frequent arbitrariness, incompetence, and ignorance of school administrators. If tenure is to be modified or removed, the method of choosing educational administrators, and the training of such administrators, must undergo salutary reform—a hard row to hoe. School administrators ought to be master teachers, not merely popular ex-coaches or empire-building bookkeepers or "experts" from educational administration centers. More and more parents are aware of the need for this parallel reform. The development of just and intelligent administrators would much diminish claims for the tenure privilege.

Teachers' Unions: What They Are and What They Might Be

Like teacher tenure, teachers' unions are a recent development, occurring principally since World War II. Until recent decades, collective bargaining was unknown in schools.

It had been assumed previously that teachers were competent to pursue their own interests without need for collective representation; and that the peculiar qualifications of an individual teacher—education and experience—would enable him to bargain competently with school boards and administrators, as most college professors do. It was taken for granted that relationships within a school generally were amicable, not adversarial, and that the school was a voluntary academic community. Teachers were viewed as partners in an educational enterprise.

All this has changed. The large majority of public primary and secondary schools in the United States have been unionized for some years. Collective bargaining, originally intended as a means for settling factory disputes, has been applied to the relationships between teachers and the institutions at which they teach.

One reason for this change has been the growth of the mass scale in public schooling. When thousands of pupils are crowded together in a vast high school, and teachers in a district or even a single "complex" may be numbered in the hundreds, personal relationships wither; it is not good to be educated in a crowd, and mass education does not warm the hearts of teachers. A crowd readily becomes a mob. Teachers who feel lost in "the lonely crowd" may hope to find solace in a union's solidarity. The inhumane scale in schooling has done much mischief in many ways since the 1950s.

Now the existence of a teachers' union does not necessarily affect for ill or for good the quality of schooling. An association or union of limited and legitimate aims, with responsible leadership and voluntary membership, may work to improve standards in a variety of aspects. But a teachers' union that is unreasonable in demands for more money, political in character, and insistent upon compulsory membership by all teachers is inimical to good schooling. The aim of such a union becomes aggrandizement, not educational improvement. This is what has happened to the National Education Association, the nation's biggest teachers' union. The NEA's political lobby in Washington and in nearly every state capital (through its affiliates) is the most formidable organized obstacle to the improvement of American schools, whether public or independent.

In an earlier stage, the National Education Association was dominated by superintendents and principals, with teachers as second-class citizens in effect. (Often the teachers had to be bullied by administrators into attending NEA affiliate meetings.) During the 1960s, control of the NEA was seized by cliques of ultraliberal or radical teachers who still remain in power.[6] At no stage was the NEA favorable to genuine educational improvement; indeed, under both dominations it has intolerantly attacked educational reformers.

The NEA's principal rival, the American Federation of Teachers with its affiliates, has been more tolerant, and indeed produces valuable publications touching on the reform of schooling. But even the AFT, detesting competition in schooling, advocates (like NEA) a virtual public school monopoly, and at present fights hard to prevent the growth of independent schools. Both big unions have strong political prejudices and alliances, although the AFT's aspirations are less radical. Both spend huge sums of money on political campaigns. The National Education Association, with 1.7 million members, spent $1.07 million on the 1982 congressional elections, up over 300 percent from the $337,000 spent on the 1980 congressional elections.

The American Federation of Teachers, with approximately half of NEA's membership, contributed $549,000 to the 1982 congressional elections, twice the $274,000 spent in the 1980 elections. Both unions said they would spend more on the 1984 elections and become active in campaign conventions.[7] Indeed, as of October 17, 1984, the NEA had spent $1,948,163 and the AFT had spent $722,027 according to a report filed with the Federal Election Commission.[8]

The NEA (and to a lesser degree, the AFT and such smaller teachers' unions as survive) impede school improvement and the development of good teachers in several ways.

First, the unions' incessant demand for higher pay has consumed, in recent years, school funds once available for special school programs, educational experiment and research, and many school amenities; any increase in school revenues has been followed promptly by demands that the money be used for higher salaries. These demands usually have been successful because of the threat of strikes—even though such strikes usually are unlawful.

Second, the NEA traditionally has set its face against "accountabil-

---

[6]"Collective Bargaining and the Freedom to Learn," *Government Union Review,* Winter 1981, pp. 34-44.
[7]"Washington News," *Education Digest,* March 1983, p. 65.
[8]Concerned Educators Against Unionism, 8001 Braddock Road, Springfield, Virginia, 22160.

ity"—that is, any system measuring teachers' ability and rewarding or dismissing accordingly. The AFT, on the other hand, consistently has agreed to examinations for teachers and is at least now willing to consider "merit pay" and other proposals for rewarding good teaching.

Third, the attachment of union leaders to political causes and candidates discriminates against teachers who do not share those views—and sometimes results in driving able teachers out of the public schools altogether. This results from compulsory membership (union shop) and compulsory dues paying in teachers' unions.

A teachers' association or union could become an instrument for "collegiality"—for bringing teachers together once more in the restoration of a focus on learning and of friendly relations within schools. It could work for effective educational reform. Confronted by public indignation at the state of the schools, even the NEA begins to make some gestures in favor of improvement.

Other Difficulties of the Teaching Profession

The maleducation of prospective teachers, the stupidities of state certification, the abuse of tenure privileges, and certain policies of teachers' unions are among the more conspicuous causes of the decay of the teaching profession. Other reasons exist.

Disorder in public schools looms large. Among the causes have been massive busing; erratic intervention into disciplinary policies by judges; students' contempt for ineffectual and "permissive" teachers; the vanishing of the vestiges of ethical instruction in the schools; and the general decline of the traditions of civility. Such conditions naturally discourage many people from entering the teaching profession. If one can do well in some other occupation, why take up a career of danger and daring, to be subjected to abuse (and sometimes abuse not verbal merely) but often denied any disciplinary authority?

Affirmative action programs enforced by federal and state governments have perplexed the schools, requiring in effect racial or ethnic quotas among teachers that take precedence over individual merits. Reverse discrimination scarcely invites able young people to become the counters of sociological games.

Enlarged opportunities for women have attracted away from teaching many well-qualified women of the sort who formerly were the permanent and experienced members of teaching staffs; and they have few successors.

To many young people who in former times would have turned to teaching as a vocation—more rewarding in the sense of duty done and personal accomplishment than as a means to "job security"— the public schools now appear to be centers for vague and unsuccessful sociological experiment, rather than pleasant communities for teaching boys and girls effectively.

Some Steps Toward Improvement

Genuinely Educating Genuine Teachers

A giant stride toward the sharp improvement of the teaching profession would be the elimination or the reform of college departments of education. This process commenced at a few universities and colleges a few years ago (for example, at Austin College in Sherman, Texas) and now is making headway—despite the American Association of Colleges for Teacher Education and the National Council for the Accreditation of Teacher Education—in some state systems and in some independent institutions.

First, departments and schools of Education should be terminated or reduced chiefly to research functions and genuine graduate studies. Their abused function of pedagogical instruction should be transferred to the several academic disciplines. Departments of physics should offer a serious course in the teaching of physics, for example, while departments of history should offer a course in methods of teaching history. Educational psychology should be included in the department of psychology; history of education in the department of history. Genuine scholars in every discipline should do what colleges and departments of Education have not been accomplishing at all well: simultaneously teaching what to teach and how to teach. This is an effective, albeit simple reform, unpopular though it would be with educationists.

Second, master teachers in elementary and secondary schools should be involved closely in the apprenticeship of beginning teachers. (This is not a new idea, but few schools in recent years have done anything about it.) Effective pedagogy cannot be taught well in the abstract by classroom lecture and textbook: it must be learned on the job.

Third, every novice teacher should understand that he is an intern, still learning under competent supervision, even though he is employed and already practicing his art. This internship should last for a year. It might well be combined with a college seminar, either during the summer or in evening hours, for exchange among the interns and general guidance by professors of academic disciplines and master teachers.

Such teaching interns would have to possess self-reliance and native intelligence; and presumably they already would have been tolerably well instructed in genuine academic disciplines, humane and scientific. The incapable would be eliminated during the internship, if not before. The capable would be heartened by this challenge to their talents.

The Reform of Certification

The present prevalent system of state certification of teachers has succeeded only in giving the nation what Secretary Bell called "teaching from the bottom": certified mediocrity, if not worse. The illusion and fraud that good teachers are produced by sitting through a good many required courses in dull Education should be swept away.

First, all aspirants to the teaching profession should be required, before entering upon internship, to pass an intelligence examination testing both their mastery of academic disciplines and their presumptive aptitude for teaching. (This examination could be administered either upon graduation from college or upon applying for a teaching post.) The examination definitely should not be drawn up by a typical department of Education. It might be prepared by one of the national testing services, a major university, or possibly competent state authorities. It should resemble the examinations of the American Medical Association, the American Bar Association and state bar associations, and other reputable professional organizations. It would be well to have a variety of such examinations available, from various sources, rather than to depend upon a single national examination. Church-related schools and other independent schools might develop their own examinations, since public institutions might exclude some studies important to such schools. Candidates for teaching who satisfactorily passed such an examination would be certified as prepared for teaching internship; the old ineffectual form of state certification would be abolished. A modified version of such a proposal, combined with the sort of internship described above, has been adopted by New Jersey. It will be administered by school districts; it will supplement, rather than supplant, the established school of education route.

Second, competence worthy of continued certification could be tested by a second examination, or successive examinations, to be administered after a period of teaching experience. These later examinations should be still more exacting; they would be far preferable to the present general insistence that teachers work in summer schools for masters' degrees in Education, or at least accumulate more boondoggle Education credits. Good teachers need more than skill in passing examinations; but such a mode of testing distinctly is superior to the present abstract instruction of teachers in classrooms.

Master Teachers, Career Ladders, Merit Pay

In almost any occupation other than teaching—even in the civil service—ordinary integrity obtains the rewards of ordinary integrity. Yet most states and school districts treat teachers as if they were identical units, of equal competence: good teachers commonly receive no recognition or reward apparently on the theory that "all animals are equal." Increase of pay usually depends solely upon seniority and accumulation of Education credits and advanced degrees (commonly Education degrees).

Yet in truth, of course, not all teachers are equal in ability and performance. Really good teachers ought to be formally recognized and rewarded, as Master Teachers, exemplars for others and supervisors of apprentice teachers.

With the concept of the Master Teacher is linked the general proposal for career ladders. In such a plan, advancement of teachers would be determined by their teaching success—not by mere accumulation of seniority and Education credits. Would this discriminatory method cause teachers not so advanced to drop out of the system? Probably; they are the deadwood that weighs down the average school. As in the case of Master Teachers, rising on the career ladder could depend upon "accountability" in the form of the academic performance of each teacher's students. Practically every other form of endeavor in America, including the churches, finds it essential to maintain the equivalent of a career ladder so as to advance those persons worthy of advancement.

Officers of teachers' unions and some teachers—particularly the mediocre—object that the policies of other occupations are not applicable to teaching. They seem to have no knowledge of the career ladders of colleges and universities with their ascending ranks of instructor, assistant professor, associate professor, and professor.

Merit pay may be joined to a career ladder or may be allocated independently: it is a plan for salary supplements for teachers and other school personnel who have served outstandingly well. Monetary reward is not the whole goal of teaching, of course; but it helps to secure competence and more than competence, just as it does in other occupations. It has been desperately unpopular with those who run teachers' unions, although some of them are beginning to give ground. Conversely, the concept of merit pay is enthusiastically applauded by the general public. Men and women in the professions are rewarded by merit pay, as well as by gratitude and public recognition. Is not teaching a profession? Or if it isn't, ought it not to become one?

Tennessee has taken the lead in merit pay, career ladders, and master teachers. In this state in 1972, some 20 percent of college freshman declared their intention of becoming teachers; today, only 4 percent of the freshmen so state. It has been estimated that 50 percent of Tennessee's first-year teachers will abandon teaching by 1990— unless some reform is worked. So, on the governor's recommendation, Tennessee's General Assembly has enacted a broad program of educational improvement that emphasizes merit pay and the career ladder. In the Tennessee career ladder program, beginning teachers are on probation their first year; then they spend three years as apprentices; they become eligible for career Level I thereafter, on passing a state-approved evaluation, and obtain tenure and a $1,000 supplement to their salaries annually. State evaluations will determine later advancement to Levels II and III. This is the most detailed and promising scheme for rewarding ability yet developed in any state, although California, Florida, and Utah already have one form or another of merit pay.

Enforced equality, regardless of merit, is enforced mediocrity— from which, as the National Commission on Excellence in Education declared, American schooling must escape. Also enforced equality is thoroughly unjust. As Aristotle put it, to treat unequal things equally is to fall into injustice. Americans have approved equality in the ultimate judgment of God and equality of treatment before the law; they distinctly have not approved enforced equality of condition and reward. And the American public now expects its schools to attract teachers who are not all equal in incompetence.

The Ends of Schooling

What educational reformers are seeking, through the programs and devices sketched above, are teachers with a sense of vocation: teachers aware that the Platonic ends of education are wisdom and virtue. The teaching profession must attract men and women who possess imagination, reason, and an eagerness to improve the minds and the consciences of the rising generation. Teachers are needed who appreciate what is called collegiality—a warm feeling of belonging to a body of colleagues who share common goals; people who recognize teaching as a high mission, who practice a vocation rather than seek to drowse in a public school sinecure. If such teachers of wisdom and virtue are to find their way into today's afflicted apparatus of public instruction, the barriers that have impeded them must be brought down.

2

Public and Private Schools

by
K. Alan Snyder

From the time of the early colonies to the conclusion of the War between the States, private schooling was the most prevalent form of education in the U.S. After the war, however, public schooling gradually gained the preeminent position it now holds. The public school system today enrolls nearly 90 percent of all American children. Yet private schools not only continue to flourish, but are becoming increasingly attractive alternatives to parents concerned about the quality of education and discipline in the public classroom.

Complaints concerning the continuing decline of Scholastic Aptitude Test scores, lack of discipline in the classroom, and the espousal of a nontraditional philosophy have turned many parents to the private school alternative. Limiting the private option, of course, are financial constraints. Parents enrolling their children in private schools pay twice for education. In recent years, however, legislation has been introduced in Congress that would lower the financial barrier to private education. Just as important, it would enhance the competition in education, producing a long overdue and beneficial challenge to the public school monopoly.

The Role of Public Schools

An early rationale for public education was espoused by Horace Mann, the "Father of the Common Schools." He sought to overcome the potential for social strife by mixing the rich and the poor in a public system that would instill each child with nonsectarian thinking.[1]

Much of what Mann said is echoed today by public school champions. The public system, they maintain, offers the best chance for equal opportunity in education for minorities and the poor. Proponents argue that the system is nonsectarian, providing an education accommodating Americans of all backgrounds and beliefs. This is true, they

---

[1] Samuel L. Blumenfeld, *Is Public Education Necessary?* (Old Greenwich, Connecticut: Devin-Adair, 1981), p. 84.

argue, because of the system's neutrality on ideological and religious issues. In addition, advocates claim that the system centers on the neighborhood and that parents are actively involved.

The truth, however, is that the public schools have added to "sectarian" segregation, that local control rarely goes beyond PTA bake sales, and that many parents are offended by the values inculcated into their children. Public schools too often now are laboratories for professional educators, who advance concepts of secular humanism.

The question to be asked today is: How can an education system meet the needs of a free and pluralist society? Perhaps an educational monopoly could have been justified in the 19th century, when people honestly believed that education would become an exact science and when there seemed to be a consensus on American values. If this were true then, it certainly is not now. Dealing with the minds of human beings as they attain knowledge is far different from working with the laws of physical science. And the steady stream of immigration has diluted the argument of value consensus considerably. The only way to meet the educational needs of diverse groups is to encourage considerable local initiative in the educational process. This will require reversing the loss of local control over education.

The history of this loss is well documented. Writes Joel Spring, Professor of Education at the University of Cincinnati: "The concern with majority determination of what should be taught in government schools began to lose meaning by the 1890s as local control began to mean elite control and professional educators gained a stronger hand over the system."[2] The composition of school boards changed; they began to be political. Professional educators, meanwhile, pressed for even more control of the system, arguing that they were above politicking and would make decisions based on the good of education only. By the 1930s, school boards had fallen so low in public esteem that suggestions were made that they be eliminated.[3]

Although school boards remain, the schools were turned over to the professional educators. Today, the idea that parents are the primary educators of their children and that they delegate this responsibility to teachers bears little resemblance to reality. The state appoints the teachers, and the parents merely accept what is provided.[4]

---

[2]Joel Spring, "The Evolving Political Structure of American Schooling," in Robert B. Everhart, ed., *The Public School Monopoly: A Critical Analysis of Education and the State in American Society* (San Francisco: Pacific Institute for Public Policy Research, 1982), p. 89.

[3]Spring, *op. cit.*, pp. 90-81; and in Lawrence Iannaccone, "Changing Political Patterns and Government Regulations," in Everhart, *op. cit.*, pp. 298-299.

[4]Philomene Di Giacomo, "Second Thoughts on the First," *Educational Freedom*, Spring-Summer 1983, p. 47.

The contention that the public schools offer a neutral, or value-free, education is also a myth. So is the alleged objectivity of the professional educator. The truth is that teaching cannot be value neutral. Choosing the texts, emphasizing key points, creating the atmosphere of the classroom and the school all convey values.[5] In a public school, rarely are decisions concerning these issues the result of parental influence. The state-planned curriculum puts its official seal of approval on certain types of literature, history, and scientific theories, and dismisses other views or interpretations. Complains concerned citizen Philomene DiGiacomo: "Academic freedom within a state school system is a contradiction in terms."[6]

Rather than being neutral, the public school system conveys values of its own. At the core of these values is secularism, placing man at the center of all things. The Supreme Court, in its 1961 *Torcaso* decision, expressly identified Secular Humanism as a religious belief.[7] So, paradoxically, in a nation where the vast majority of citizens believe in God, the public schools promote a religious concept without a God. At the very least, the humanistic commitment of the public schools fails to meet America's pluralistic needs.

When the educators took control of the system, the old politics based in city wards was replaced by a politics of the educated elite. This is, writes Lawrence Iannaccone, Professor of Education at the University of California, Santa Barbara, "a thoroughgoing apologia for the power of the strong, professional, bureaucratic state."[8]

The most political of the professional education groups is the National Education Association (NEA). Since its transformation in the early 1970s from an organization concerned mainly with the working conditions of teachers to one centered on political activism, NEA membership has grown beyond that of any other public employee union; it trails only the Teamsters in total members. Although it suffered very serious political setbacks in the 1984 elections, the NEA still wields political clout. What is more, the NEA takes a radical stance on most issues.

As to the claim that public schools offer the best chance for the poor and minorities, recent studies have indicated that they do not. Public education policy in recent decades has led to even greater discrimination against these groups, via forced busing and the resultant "white

---

[5]Stephen Arons and Charles Lawrence III, "The Manipulation of Consciousness: A First Amendment Critique of Schooling," in Everhart, *op. cit.*, p. 231.

[6]Di Giacomo, *op. cit.*, p. 43.

[7]John W. Whitehead and John Conlan, "The Establishment of the Religion of Secular Humanism and Its First Amendment Implications," *Educational Freedom*, Fall-Winter 1980-1981, p. 9.

[8]Iannaccone, *op. cit.*, p. 311.

flight," for instance. Statistics show that public schools are becoming more segregated, while private schools are growing more integrated.[9] Many children from upper-middle and upper class families now attend essentially segregated public schools in the suburbs. This leaves the inner-city minority child locked in an often deteriorating, one-race, inner-city public school. Minority parents who want the best for their children are making the sacrifices to send them to academically superior, more disciplined private schools. Indeed, minorities accounted for 20.4 percent of the 1982-83 Catholic school enrollments. And minority enrollments in the private schools in general have nearly doubled during the last ten years.[10]

The stated goals of the public school system—educational opportunity for the poor and minorities, nonsectarianism, and local control—clearly are not being realized.

The Role of Private Schools

For the most part, private schools have been able to attain greater academic quality, generate more concern for moral values, and offer a generally better disciplined classroom atmosphere than have public schools. Private education continues to exist because of the demand for its services. It meets the needs of a pluralistic U.S. because parents exercise more influence over its policies and because it combines high academic achievement and respect for traditional moral and spiritual values.

The largest share of private school students attend Roman Catholic schools. They originally were founded to provide an alternative to the Protestant public education establishment. Nowadays, however, it is the Protestants who are opening up hundreds of new private schools each year, in response to what they believe is a public school system adrift in moral and academic relativism. Again, the rationale is for choice. The possibilities are almost unlimited; there is opportunity for any group to further its own precepts. Such flexibility is not available in the public sector.

Private school parents feel more like a part of their children's education. As a Catholic League study of Catholic inner-city schools

---

[9]Thomas W. Vitullo-Martin, "The Impact of Taxation Policy on Public and Private Schools," in Everhart, *op. cit.,* pp. 446-447.

[10]The Advisory Panel on Financing Elementary and Secondary Education's Comments on the School Finance Project, prepared by Dr. Vitullo-Martin, consultant, April 29, 1984, p. 17 (available from the Chairman's Office, Free Congress Foundation, 721 Second Street, N.E., Washington, D.C., 20002).

reveals, a primary reason for parents to send their children to private school is that they feel the school officials are more responsive.[11]

Independent, fundamentalist Christian schools, consistently show greater academic progress at all grade levels. Two large Christian school organizations, the Association of Christian Schools International (ACSI) and the American Association of Christian Schools (AACS), make an annual accounting of their students' scores on the Stanford Achievement test and compare the results with those of the public schools. The 1982-83 results for ACSI reveal that its students placed higher than public school students in each grade. The smallest difference was in the first grade; there ACSI pupils were five months ahead of their public counterparts. From here on, the gap steadily widens until ninth grade where the differential is sixteen months.[12] The AACS results are similar.[13]

With regard to moral values and discipline, 90 percent of America's private schools are religious in nature. Parents can be confident that the Judeo-Christian tradition will be dominant, in contrast to the general public school pattern of a curriculum based upon secular humanism.

In spite of their record of solid achievement, private schools have suffered since the mid-1960s. As inflation pushed up costs faster than incomes, as the birth rate fell, and as centralized welfare policies alienated urban middle and upper income families, private school enrollments declined.

Catholic schools, which were concentrated in the inner cities, suffered the greatest loss when their constituents fled to the suburbs. Between 1965 and 1978, 3,500 Catholic schools closed. Catholic school systems lost two million students, some 40 percent of their student population.[14] This rate of decrease has slowed, but now Catholic schools account for only 64 percent of private school enrollment, as compared to 87 percent before the decline started.[15]

Other denominations, however, increased enrollment. Lutheran, Episcopal, and Jewish schools doubled enrollments during this period. Baptist schools increased their enrollments nine fold.[16] Collec-

---

[11]*Inner City Private Education: A Study* (Milwaukee: The Catholic League for Religious and Civil Rights, 1982), p. 13.
[12]ACSI 1982-1983 Stanford Achievement Test Scores.
[13]AACS 1982-1983 Stanford Achievement Test Scores.
[14]Roger A. Freeman, "Educational Tax Credits," in Everhart, *op. cit.*, p. 474.
[15]Rev. Msgr. Vincent D. Breen, "Tuition Tax Credits," *The Journal of the Institute for Socioeconomic Studies,* Spring 1984, p. 22.
[16]*United States Catholic Elementary and Secondary Schools 1983-1984: A Statistical Report on School Enrollment and Staffing* (Washington, D.C.: The National Catholic Education Association, 1984), p. 4.

tively, these denominations accounted for nearly one-third of nonpublic enrollment.[17] In addition, there has been a dramatic increase in independent fundamentalist schools, especially since the 1970s. This partly is a reaction to declining public school achievement scores. Mainly, however, it seems that many parents believe public schools are hostile toward the Judeo-Christian view of a civilized, educated society. Currently, there is no accurate count of these Christian schools, many of whom desire to stay as unnoticed as possible because of fear of government pressure to conform to secular education.

The fact that private school enrollment now seems to be on the rise means that parents are making this choice despite the financial burden of paying twice for education—once in the form of taxes for the public system and again in the form of private school tuition. This burden has led to calls for government action to ensure the well-being of private education.

How Government Involvement Affects Private Education

State governments became extensively involved in curriculum and in training and licensing teachers by the 1930s. Teachers at public schools now have to pass certain courses prescribed by the state and to be certified by the state.[18] The federal government entered the education picture with the passage of the National Defense Education Act of 1958.[19]

Washington uses three methods to influence schools: direct regulation, categorical grants, and the tax codes.[20] Direct regulation is used primarily in aid to the disadvantaged and the handicapped; categorical grants earmark federal funds for certain subjects, thereby shutting out input from local educators; tax codes determine what are and are not acceptable tax deductions for educational purposes. Private schools are more affected by these codes than by direct regulation or categorical grants.

Private schools have been the beneficiaries of only a small amount of government aid. Some schools, mainly Catholic and Lutheran, participate in the Title I/Chapter I (of the Elementary and Secondary Education Act) and handicapped programs. But the majority of

---

[17]Freeman, *op. cit.*, p. 474.
[18]Spring, *op. cit.*, p.93.
[19]*Ibid.*, p. 97.
[20]Vitullo-Martin, *op. cit.*, pp. 425-426.

private schools are very wary of government ties. They are concerned that they will become entangled in a web of government regulations that could strangle their educational philosophies, force them into expensive affirmative action programs, require teachers to submit to state certification, and mandate curriculum content. Judging by the treatment many of these schools receive at the hands of the Internal Revenue Service, there is good reason for concern.

An incident in the late 1970s convinced a significant segment of the private school educators that educational freedom could become a victim of federal control. Following a U.S. District Court decision, which held that the IRS should withhold tax-exempt status from private schools in Mississippi that had been found to discriminate, the IRS issued a ruling that all U.S. tax-exempt private schools had to declare a nondiscrimination policy or lose their tax-exempt status. Over 99 percent of the schools did so.

Then civil rights lawyers persuaded the IRS that private schools founded after 1954, the start of mandated integration, should prove that they were not discriminatory. Using outcome as proof of intent, in August 1978, the IRS proposed regulations requiring a quota system for minority students. Example: if a school was in a locale that was 20 percent black, it was expected that 20 percent of its enrollment would be black. If not, the school was required to promote its availability to black students and work to bring the enrollment up to the quota. If it did not, it could lose its tax exemption.

These proposed regulations drew protest unprecedented in the history of IRS regulations. The reason: the regulations were declaring a school guilty until proved innocent. The IRS, in effect, was declaring that schools founded since 1954 were designed to avoid the racial intergration required of public schools. The IRS ignored the fact that many of these schools were founded to meet the needs of the members of their churches; student populations at such schools, reflecting the composition of their congregations, obviously would not have the prescribed quota of minorities. The regulations did not take this into account. Hearings were held by the House Ways and Means Committee in 1979, and Congress then acted to prohibit the IRS from enforcing any new regulations over private schools.[21] Though this action eliminated the immediate threat, the government was viewed with more suspicion than before. Private schools, therefore, are on guard against regulatory efforts.

---

[21]Jeremy Rabkin, "Educational Choice vs. Racial Regulation: Non-Discrimination Safeguards and the Tuition Tax Credit Bill," issue paper published by LEARN, Inc., Washington, D.C., pp. 5-10.

How Should Government Aid Private Schools?

There are basically two types of financial aid to private school parents currently under consideration: tuition tax credits and vouchers. Either would help low- and middle-income parents afford private education and also would limit government involvement.

Tuition Tax Credits

Proposals for tuition tax credits are similar in form to the present child care credit. Tuition tax credits would be subtracted directly from the amount of tax owed by a parent after all other deductions have been figured. The purpose is to give relief to families who send their children to private schools but are discouraged from doing so because of the tuition burden. The rationale is that it is unfair for parents to have to pay tuition for a private school in addition to taxes for public schools. This is a particularly heavy burden for the poor and a large segment of the middle class. Write Professors Arons and Lawrence: "In effect, we confront the dissenting family with a choice between giving up its basic values as the price of gaining a 'free' education in a government school or paying twice in order to preserve its First Amendment rights."[22]

Senator Daniel P. Moynihan, the New York Democrat, notes that the U.S. is the only industrial democracy in the world that does not provide aid to nonpublic schools.[23] Tuition tax credits appear to be an acceptable form of aid to nearly all the private schools, the fundamentalists included.[24] Recent legislative proposals allow families to receive federal tax credits for half the tuition paid to a private, tax-exempt elementary or secondary school (with a maximum of $300 per child).

The NEA has denounced tuition tax credit legislation as "the most dangerous threat in the history of public education." It would imperil, claims NEA, "the entire existing federal financial contribution to public education." The aim of the legislation, adds NEA, is to weaken

---

[22]Arons and Lawrence, *op. cit.*, pp. 237-238.
[23]Daniel P. Moynihan, "What Congress Can Do When the Court is Wrong," in Edward McGlynn Gaffney, Jr., ed., *Private Schools and the Public Good: Policy Alternatives for the Eighties* (University of Notre Dame Press, 1981), p. 92.
[24]Dr. Ron Johnson, Vice President of Accelerated Christian Education, one of the most fundamental Christian school organizations in the country, noted that tuition tax credits would be identical to child care, care for the elderly, and energy savings credits, and that his association could support such legislation. Citizens for Education Freedom press release, February 18, 1983.

the public school system by diverting public funds for private education.[25] The NEA is waging a battle against all forms of aid to private schools. It has been joined by the National Coalition for Public Education, Americans United for the Separation of Church and State, the American Jewish Committee, and the Public Education and Religious Liberty Association.[26]

They fear that attendance by more children at private schools could cripple the public system. Noted scholar Roger Freeman explains, however, that tuition tax credits would not start a stampede to private schools because the financial burden would not be removed, only lowered somewhat. He stresses that only if private schools were allowed to be more competitive could public schools feel the competition to make changes for the better. As such, tuition tax credit legislation could benefit both private and public education.[27]

At issue, too, is the proper mode of education. Observes Roger Freeman:

> The basic question was and is whether all, or almost all, children should receive their education in government-run schools or whether there should be diversity of offerings, giving parents a choice in the type of education they wish their children to receive and in the school they want them to attend.[28]

Broadly speaking, there are three recurring arguments against tuition tax credits: discrimination, the First Amendment, and the budget.

Discrimination: It is alleged that the majority of private schools are in some way tainted with racist ideas. Private education is supposed to be the haven for "white flight" and for the elite and wealthy. These concerns, however, are not supported by the data.

Census records from the 1978-1979 school year reveal that 62.7 percent of families with children in private schools had incomes under $25,000; 45.6 percent under $20,000; 27 percent under $15,000; 11.2 percent under $10,000. In the inner cities, an astounding 72 percent of families with children in private school earned under $15,000.[29] Obviously, private schools attract parents from across the economic spectrum.

Even in very expensive schools there are opportunities for the

---

[25]*NEA Reporter,* May-June 1978, pp. 1-2.
[26]Daniel B. McGarry, "The Advantages and Constitutionality of Tuition Tax Credits," *Educational Freedom,* Spring-Summer 1982, p. 1; Interim Report of the Governors' Legislative Committee on Nonpublic Schools, March 1981.
[27]Freeman, *op. cit.,* p. 471.
[28]*Ibid.,* pp. 486-487.
[29]McGarry, *op. cit,* p. 13.

financially disadvantaged. Statistics compiled by the National Association of Independent Schools, under whose umbrella can be found some of the most expensive schools in America, indicate that its member schools gave scholarships to 16 percent of their students in 1980.[30]

The study also surveyed Catholic and Lutheran school enrollment and found that both systems are becoming less segregated. Catholic schools enroll a higher percentage of Hispanics than do the public schools; Lutherans enroll a higher percentage of blacks. In 1978, the Lutheran Church-Missouri Synod schools, the most conservative Lutheran schools, had 12.5 percent minority enrollment in their elementary grades and 16.3 percent in secondary; only 2 percent of the church's membership is black.[31]

A presidential advisory panel that released its findings in May 1984 suggests that low-income Americans are most likely to benefit from tuition tax credit legislation. Only 3 percent of families with incomes over $25,000 indicated they would switch their children to private schools because of a tax credit, whereas 20 percent of blacks and Hispanics said that they would be inclined to switch under the same circumstances.[32]

The First Amendment: Are tuition tax credits constitutional?

The first case to challenge government subsidies of church-related education was *Everson* (1947). There, the Court approved state reimbursement of parents of children in nonpublic schools for costs of transportation, stating that since the aid went to the parents, not the schools, it did not violate the Constitution's establishment clause ensuring separation of church and state. To this decision, however, Justice Hugo Black wrote an opinion calling for a wall of separation between church and state that was to remain "high and impregnable." He asserted that government cannot pass laws that "aid one religion, aid all religions, or prefer one religion over another."[33]

Yet the Founding Fathers apparently did not intend to prevent aid to religion in general. The Congress had already granted such aid through the terms of the Northwest Ordinance of 1787, which stated, "Religion, morality, and knowledge being necessary to good government and the happiness of mankind, schools and the means of education shall forever be encouraged." After passage of the First Amendment, Congress provided lands for churches in the West, subsidized missionaries among the Indians, and maintained chap-

---

[30]Vitullo-Martin, *op. cit.*, p. 445.
[31]*Ibid.*, pp. 446-447.
[32]"Study Supports Private School Tax Credit," *The Washington Times,* May 1, 1984.
[33]McGarry, *op. cit.*, p. 17.

lains in the armed forces. In addition, many states made grants to private schools, most of which were church-related.[34]

After years of tortuous debate over the constitutionality of tuition tax relief, the Supreme Court finally has ruled in its favor. In the 1983 *Mueller* case, the Court supported the constitutionality of educational tax deductions by the state of Minnesota.[35]

The Budget: NEA argues that tuition tax credits would deny the federal government needed funds. This assumes that a tax deduction is the same thing as a subsidy, even though this was denied by the *Mueller* ruling. Notes Larry Uzzell, president of LEARN, Inc.:

> Unless we accept the view that all income rightly belongs to the government, we must reject the proposition that there is no moral or economic distinction between policies which let people keep their own earnings and policies which grant them the earning of others. To refrain from stealing my sandwich is not the same thing as giving me a free lunch.[36]

Even if all the tax deductions for public and private schools were treated as subsidies, current tuition tax credit proposals would not tip the balance in favor of private schools. Based upon 1985 projections, the federal government's "subsidy" for each public school student would be $517. The Treasury Department estimates that the 1985 revenue loss caused by tuition tax credits would have been $1 billion. If this were divided by the projected five million private school students, the federal help would amount to only $200 per student. Admittedly, these are conservative figures because they do not take into account bonds and direct grants from government agencies to public schools; neither do they account for the number of private school students who would not receive the tuition tax credit because their parents' earnings were over the maximum limit.[37]

Yet the entire question of the expense involved with tuition tax credits is misleading: for each child attending a private school, the taxpaying public enjoys a smaller tax burden; one less child in the public classroom means lower government outlays and hence lower taxes. If all private schools were closed and their students headed for public schools, state and local taxes would have to be raised at least $11 billion. In reality, says Roger Freeman, "tax credits would cause public expenditures to drop several times as much as revenues. Tax credits come at a profit to public treasuries not as a loss."[38]

---

[34]*Ibid.,* p. 38.
[35]McGarry, "The Mueller v. Allen Case (1983)," *Education Freedom,* Spring-Summer 1983, pp. 1-5.
[36]Lawrence A. Uzzell, "Issue Brief: Tuition Tax Credits," LEARN, Inc., undated, p. 1.
[37]*Ibid.,* pp. 1-4.
[38]Freeman, *op. cit.,* p. 488.

Tuition tax credits can only help American education: they will lessen the injustice of double taxation for private school parents; they will help private education survive and provide healthy competition and points of comparison for public schools; they will foster parental choice and personal freedom; they will help turn U.S. education away from the establishment of secular humanism; and they will be cost effective, creating no new bureaucracy, but merely adding a line on the federal income tax form.[39]

Vouchers

Another form of education aid for private schools is the voucher system. Vouchers generally could be used in whatever school a parent chose, public or private. Under this plan, parents would receive a voucher to pay for the cost of education in the school district. The parents would decide whether to use the voucher in a private or a public school. This gives maximum choice to all parents and puts schools on notice that unless they offer a decent product they will lose students. In this way the best schools, whether public or private, would receive the most students and also receive the money for educating those students.

This plan would follow the Supreme Court's strictures against direct aid to private schools, because the parents would be the aid recipients; schools would be aided only to the extent that parents chose them. Schools would have to provide the education sought by the parents. Many tuition tax credit proponents actually view tax credit legislation as a stop-gap measure and look forward to a voucher system.[40]

The federal government's Office of Economic Opportunity (OEO) in the early 1970s tried a voucher experiment in a California school district. This plan, however, had several huge drawbacks: teachers were not rewarded for increased enrollments, and poor teachers were assured of job security; parental choice was limited by placing enrollment lids on some schools; private schools were not included. This prevented the OEO experiment from being a valid test of vouchers. Additionally, the OEO tried to set up another bureaucracy to distribute the vouchers, provide information to parents, and monitor school quality.[41]

---

[39]McGarry, "The Advantages and Constitutionality of Tax Credits," pp. 4-9.
[40]Interview with Sister Renee Oliver, February, 29, 1984.
[41]E.G. West, "The Prospects for Education Vouchers: An Economic Analysis," in Everhart, *op. cit.,* p. 383.

Some scholars point to the British Columbia assistance program (begun in 1978) as a more valid test. In this "voucher" experiment, however, assistance was given directly to the public and private schools. In his study of Canadian private schools in British Columbia, Donald Erickson concluded that, after the initiation of direct government assistance, the schools ceased to be close-knit communities with shared goals and personal commitments. No longer did the private schools seem special in any way. They became clones of the public schools. Erickson concluded that such changes "might not have occurred if the private schools had been 'aided' not by grants given directly to the schools themselves, but by vouchers or tax credits to parents."[42]

A successful voucher system has been in operation in Vermont since the early 1800s. There, the local governments use tax revenues to pay for the parents' choice of public or private education for their children. Vermont's program poses some problems. First, if tuition at a private school exceeds that of the average Vermont union (public) school, parents generally are expected to pay the difference. Thus, inequalities exist in the types of schools students can afford to attend. Second, Vermont vouchers apply only to those nonsectarian private schools approved by the Vermont Department of Education. This aspect of the program would trigger strong opposition from religious groups. Nevertheless, Vermont's program is a testament to the viability of the voucher concept.

The criticisms leveled at tuition tax credits are repeated in connection with voucher programs. And the answers are virtually the same. If expanded choice for parents via tuition tax credits leads to greater integration, and indications are that it would, then so it would with vouchers, probably to a greater extent. The constitutionality of vouchers would seem in line with the Supreme Court verdict on Minnesota's tuition tax deductions, particularly because the payments are made to parents and not to the schools. In respect to the fiscal soundness of the system, budgets are already in place, and all that would be necessary would be to transfer the money directly to the parents.

Rather than just a reduction in taxes, a voucher would pay the entire school bill. Even if all the private school cost could not be covered, the tuition left for parents to pay would be minimal, and the opportunity would open up for many who are now unable to cover the cost of a private school, since private schools have a lower per pupil expense than public schools.

---

[42]Donald A. Erickson, "Disturbing Evidence About the 'One Best System,'" in Everhart, *op. cit.*, p. 419.

A voucher system would not require much regulation; it could be laissez-faire in approach or include some regulatory safeguards.[43] A system that would forbid government involvement in curriculum choices, teacher certification, and school accreditation should be acceptable to even the most fundamentalist Christian school.

Vouchers are most promising on the state level, since the federal government provides only about 6 percent of the nation's education bill. The Reagan Administration has proposed initiating vouchers for the Chapter I program for the educationally disadvantaged. The proposal is stalled in Congress, but if given a chance, it could test how well the voucher can work in an open market situation.

Conclusion

Private schools antedated public education in the U.S. Today, they offer an alternative to a purely secular approach. Their vitality, however, is seriously undermined by a tax code that encourages reliance on the public system. Tuition tax credits or vouchers would bring a measure of equity for parents: tuition tax credits would ease the burden for those paying private school tuition; vouchers would go a step farther and use current taxes to grant parents freedom of choice. Neither discrimination, constitutionality, nor budgetary considerations hold up as arguments against either option. It is time for these issues to be dropped and debate to be focused on the real merits of both proposals. If professional educators are serious about improving education in general, they will have to acknowledge the benefits that tuition tax credits and vouchers can bring to all schools, private as well as public.

---

[43]John E. Coons and Stephen D. Sugarman, "Credits v. Subsidies: Comment on the California Tuition Tax Credit Proposal," in Gaffney, *op. cit.*, pp. 106-113.

3

The Growth of the Federal Role in Education

by
Eileen M. Gardner

During the past quarter century, the federal government has claimed unprecedented control over U.S. education policy. Regulations and mandates attached to the receipt of federal dollars have been the primary vehicles for this growth. These rules derive from federal aid programs that redirect state and local education priorities, skew balanced instructional programs, and create unnecessary and undesirable administrative bureaucracies.

Much has been written about the agenda of the federal education bureaucracy. Well-documented criticisms of this agenda, however, have failed to influence federal education legislation, partly because federal education policy decisions remain rooted in assumptions unresponsive to data that disprove them. Some of these assumptions are:

1) equality of opportunity is synonymous with equality of result. Failure to attain equality of result must, therefore, be due to discrimination;

2) the "state" has the duty to equalize the inequalities of result;

3) since social conditioning shapes man's nature, and since man creates social conditions, then man himself determines what he will be. Equality of result, then, can be obtained through altering stimuli;

4) parents, local education agencies, and state education agencies cannot be trusted; in the past these groups have ignored the needs of the "disadvantaged," the handicapped, the limited-English-proficient, and women; therefore education must be policed by the federal government to protect the rights of these "underserved" populations.

Because those attempting to point out the fallacies in these assumptions have no organized power base, federal education legislation has been largely impervious to their criticisms. In too many instances, special interests have pressed Congress into creating programs based on these false premises. Congressional committee structure, in turn, has accommodated and advanced the special interest agendas. Individual Members, for instance, adopt a single issue and fight to preserve and to further it, often at the expense of the welfare of the whole. This has left the ordinary American without a lobby group or Congressional Member to represent his interests in education (such policies as protect the general welfare). Thus, subsidiary agendas supersede the main fare without substantive opposition.

Between 1963 and 1965 serious racial strife directed the nation's attention to the poor, academically slow student. Many saw the schools as the means through which poverty and inequality could be eradicated and equality of result achieved. Such outcomes came to be viewed as a civil right. President Lyndon Johnson told a Howard University audience on June 4, 1965:

> You do not take a person who, for years, has been hobbled by chains and liberate him, bring him up to the starting line of a race and then say, "You are free to compete with all the others," and still justly believe that you have been completely fair.... It is not enough just to open the gates of opportunity. All our citizens must have the ability to walk through those gates.... This is the next and the more profound stage of the battle for civil rights. We seek not just freedom but opportunity. We seek not just legal equity but human ability, not just equality as a right and a theory but equality as a fact and equality as a result.... To this end equal opportunity is essential, but not enough, not enough.[1]

Federal priorities shifted from basic skills and excellence to basic access and remediation. The Johnson landslide of 1964 set the stage for massive federal aid to and involvement in the affairs of elementary and secondary schools. The following year saw passage of the Elementary and Secondary Education Act (ESEA). Title I of this Act provides federal aid to counties for compensatory (remedial) education for educationally disadvantaged students from low-income families.[2] In 1966, Title VI, targeting education for handicapped children,

---

[1] Quoted in Diane Ravitch, *The Troubled Crusade: American Education 1945-1980* (New York: Basic Books, Inc., 1983), p. 154.

[2] Titles II through V of the ESEA were largely interest group appeasement grant programs. Several became the vehicles for direct federal involvement in local education affairs: Title II, which provided grants to states for school library resources, textbooks, and other instructional materials for public and private elementary schools, pleased parochial school supporters. Title III, which provided funds for supplementary educational centers and services, appealed to educational reformers in the 1960s who wished to overhaul traditional school practices (criticized as being based on middle-class values unresponsive to the equalitarian sentiment of the day); reform was to be effected through direct federal approval authority over, and grants to support, local educational "innovations." Title IV broadened federal authority over educational research through direct federal grants to university connected research centers and autonomous regional educational agencies. This latter appeased state officials unhappy with being by-passed in several areas by the federal government in dealing with local education agencies. See Stephen Bailey and Edith Mosher, "ESEA: The Office of Education Administers a Law" (Syracuse University Press, 1968), pp. 52-58.

was added to ESEA.[3] In 1968, Title VII, the Bilingual Education Act, was added. Then, in 1974, came Title IX, the Women's Educational Equity Act.

Title I: Compensatory Education

Social engineers have argued that inequalities would not exist if the social structure were changed. In keeping with this approach, Title I was formulated on the assumption that social deprivation causes the generally poor academic performance of minority students from low-income families and that this can be overcome by concentrated remediation. This assumption ignores the fact that academic ability is tied inexorably to basic intelligence. If, as these same social engineers generally argue, it is their dismal home environment that mainly explains the low IQ scores of slow learners, then concentrated remediation cannot bring the academic capability of an individual with low intelligence up to that of his average IQ peers. This assumption also ignores the evidence that expenditures on education cannot raise substantially such a student's level of academic performance.

Title I has been funded ebulliently—from the deluded enthusiasm at its inception through the somber realization of its failure. Nearly $1 billion was appropriated for Title I in FY 1966, its first year of funding. The $2.7 billion appropriated in FY 1978 represented some 47 percent of all federal elementary and secondary spending.[4] Congress appropriated $3.48 billion for FY 1984. To date, cumulative federal spending for compensatory education has been over $42 billion.[5]

Studies assessing the effectiveness of Title I consistently have shown that the goal of the program has never been achieved. Yet Congress steadfastly has resisted efforts to eliminate it. By 1969, however, clear signals were reaching Capitol Hill that Title I was failing to live up to its expectations. Results of congressionally mandated evaluations showed that federal budget officials did not view the program as cost effective; educators complained of red tape, excessive regulations, and unwieldy bureaucracy; and parents of eligible children complained they saw little change in the quality of

---

[3]The Education for the Handicapped Act of 1970 replaced Title VI of ESEA. Title VI later became Impact Aid.

[4]Report of the Committee on Governmental Affairs, United States Senate, to Accompany S. 991 to Establish a Department of Education and For Other Purposes, Together With Additional Views, Report No. 95-1078, May 17, 1978.

[5]U.S. Department of Education, Office of the Budget, Washington, D.C.

their children's education.[6] Most telling, perhaps, the achievement test scores of the children served were not significantly better than their non-Title I counterparts. The small improvements they did make proved temporary.

Congressional liberals, unable to point to examples of Title I's success, were embarrassed by these findings,[7] but philosophical backers of Title I argued that test scores were not necessarily relevant in assessing the program's success. Improved self-concept and access, they asserted, might be more important than academic outcome. Others pointed to what they claimed was inadequate funding, poor funding distribution, and nontargeted funds as the primary culprits in the disappointing results. During the 1970s, then, Congress focused on increasing access to Title I services and ensuring they reached those for whom they were intended.

In 1975, the U.S. Office of Education funded "A Study of the Sustaining Effects of Compensatory Education on Basic Cognitive Skills." It was one of the largest studies of elementary education in U.S. history. The overriding conclusions of the achievement section of the study, released in 1981, indicated that, while the high achieving Title I-eligible students benefitted from one-year exposure to remedial work, by and large, slow students stayed slow students. Indeed, by the time they entered junior high school, no benefit from Title I was observable.[8]

Oddly, these data had no noticeable effect on Congress's views of the program. High levels of funding continued. In fact, by the early 1980s, public policy was forcing researchers to distort data. A prime example is a 1982 report by the congressionally mandated National Assessment of Educational Progress (NAEP)[9] on the reading, science, and mathematics performance of American youth during the 1970s. No grade levels were given; no standardized tests were used. Peformance on subjective "exercises" created by "specialists" determined "achievement classes." "Lowest" and "highest" were insufficiently defined. No objective criteria for reclassification from one

---

[6]"Intergovernmentalizing the Classroom: Federal Involvement in Elementary and Secondary Education," in *The Federal Role in the Federal System: The Dynamics of Growth* (Washington, D.C.: Advisory Commission on Intergovernmental Relations, March 1981), p. 44.

[7]Frederick M. Wirt and Michael W. Kirst, *The Political Web of American Schools* (Boston, Massachusetts: Little, Brown, and Co., 1972), p. 153.

[8]"A Study of Compensatory and Elementary Education: The Sustaining Effects Study," Final Report, Launor F. Carter, Project Director from 1975-1981. Prepared by the System Development Corporation for the Office of Program Evaluation, U.S. Department of Education, January 1983.

[9]"Reading, Science and Mathematics Trends: A Closer Look," National Assessment of Education Progress, December 1982.

group to another were given. Vague data for Title I eligible schools were given, but Title I students were not identified.

Contradictions were unclarified. On the one hand, students within Title I eligible schools were reported to have increased their representation in mathematics and science in the highest achievement class at age nine and to have decreased their representation in the lowest achieving math class at age seventeen. However, a separate chart dividing groups into lowest and highest achievers showed that the lowest achievers at ages nine and thirteen significantly improved in reading but made no significant progress in math (nine and thirteen) and science (nine). At seventeen, the lowest achievers had declined in math, as well as reading, and had made no progress in science.

Congress has used the data on the reading of nine- and thirteen-year-old low achievers to justify continued high funding levels for compensatory education. Yet there is no indication that the reading improvement resulted from Title I efforts, since the percentage of Title I students in the lowest achiever group was not presented and since the Title I data that were presented show no significant movement out of the lowest achievement or into the highest achievement classes in reading. The whole issue may be moot, however, since by the age of seventeen, either no growth or regression is shown.

Most recently, Stephen P. Mullen of the University of Pennsylvania and Anita A. Summers of the Wharton School of Business published the findings of an evaluation of 47 studies on the overall effectiveness of compensatory education. Their findings:

* the results of most studies are overstated because of the upward biases inherent in several standard statistical procedures;

* the gains appear to be greater in earlier years, [but] the evidence is fairly strong that early gains are not sustained;

* no significant association exists between dollars spent and achievement gains.[10]

Even if the premise is accepted that reading gains have been effected by Title I participation, the quality of those gains is suspect. Researchers are quick to point out that the reading gains of the lowest achievers have not been of a cognitive nature. Lower level decoding skills, not higher level cognitive skills, account for the registered gain. (This would explain the decline in the reading skills of the older low achievers, who would face reading tasks of an almost purely cognitive nature.)

These most modest "gains" of the educationally slower student, then, appear to be temporary and noncognitive in nature. Worse, the

---

[10]Stephen P. Mullen and Anita A. Summers, "Is More Better? The Effectiveness of Spending on Compensatory Education," *Phi Delta Kappan,* January 1983, p. 339.

mammoth effort expended to achieve them probably was at the expense of the average and academically talented student. Between 1967 and 1975, for instance, the number of students scoring above 700 (of a possible 800) on the mathematics section of the Scholastic Aptitude Test (SAT) declined by 15 percent.[11] From 1979 to 1980 alone, the number of students scoring over 750 in either the verbal or the mathematics section of the SAT fell from 2,650 to 1,892 (verbal) and from 9,059 to 7,675 (mathematics).[12] Additional data from the National Assessment of Education Progress show that the highest achievers significantly declined in science and mathematics performance during the 1970s, most often at two and three times the mean change upward of the lowest achievers.

These findings should be of no surprise to those who have observed the changed focus in education over the past two decades. At the same time that it began to be clear that compensatory education was not producing the desired result, during the late 1960s and early 1970s, the education establishment discredited any measures that would indicate its failure: Standardized tests were called "elitist" and "culturally biased"; academic rigor in schools was maligned; academic standards were lowered or eliminated altogether; substantive academic courses were replaced by courses of highly questionable merit.

Further indication of the negative impact on focusing on the less able students comes from a small but significant study in Pinellas County, Florida, in which the researchers concluded that the modest gains by slower students during the past twenty years possibly were at the cost of the above average achievers.[13]

In summary, Title I has not achieved the goal for which it was established; it has consumed some $42 billion in taxpayer's money over eighteen years with little lasting effect. Yet, remarkably, it has continued to enjoy a high level of congressional support.

Education of the Handicapped

Until the 1930s, the concept of responsibility for oneself and one's family was a cornerstone of American society. In addition, most willingly shared in the care of neighbors in need. Then during the Great Depression, the federal government, for humanitarian reasons, began to do for individuals what they could not do for themselves.

---

[11] Fact Sheet from the National Convention in Precollege Education in Mathematics and Science, May 12-13, 1982 (Washington, D.C.: National Science Foundation).

[12] Solveig Eggerz, *Why Our Public Schools are Failing and What We Must Do About It* (New Rochelle, New York: America's Future, 1982).

[13] Jane Elligett and Thomas S. Tocco, "Reading Achievement in 1979 v. Achievement in the Fifties," *Phi Delta Kappan,* June 1980, pp. 698-699.

Thus began what is now an almost total involvement of the federal government in areas previously the responsibility of the individual, the family, the community, and the state.

One extreme manifestation of this is Washington's insistence that it has the primary responsibility to oversee the care of the handicapped. Yet national government is ill-suited for this task. Broad mandates that impose rigid standards and procedures cannot effectively prescribe for the hundreds of existing handicapping conditions. In addition, they dull America's traditional sense of mutual obligation and charity and the resultant capacity for innovative local solutions. Personal giving and flexible accommodations have been replaced by an impersonal, and at times adversarial, system.

The goal of those advocating federal responsibility for the handicapped has been to integrate the handicapped child fully into the social and educational mainstream and to erase all "meaningful" differences between him and other children. Yet a blind child has restrictions that a seeing child does not have, and a retarded child will never attain the mental acuity or the social sophistication of a nonretarded child. Endless aid and regulations will not erase these undeniable differences. In an apparent refusal to accept this fact, the lobby for the handicapped has pushed proposals that have been a disservice to the nonhandicapped population. The "learning disability" category, for instance, is a vague term that has caused the mislabeling, stigmatizing, and fragmented education of many normal children, yet it remains in the federal definition of a handicap and in the federal funding formula.

The Campaign

The 1954 Supreme Court decision in *Brown v. Board of Education* had a profound impact on subsequent legislation and court decisions regarding the handicapped. Linking education of the handicapped with civil rights arguments, the handicap lobby insisted that separate treatment of handicapped children in itself is discriminatory. Using the precedent of Title VI of the 1964 Civil Rights Act (empowering federal officials to withhold funds from programs violating antidiscrimination laws and regulations), lobbyists for the handicapped pushed Washington to make the states guarantee their definition of a free and appropriate education for all handicapped children as a civil right.

Federal control of education for the handicapped has grown steadily. In 1966 Congress added Title VI—Education of the Handicapped—to the Elementary and Secondary Education Act (ESEA). Between 1967 and 1968, authorizations for Title VI tripled from $50 million to $150 million. Centralized control was extended, largely through increasing specificity of the legislation. In 1970, the Education for the Handicapped Act was passed, replacing Title VI of ESEA.

Emboldened by success at the congressional level, the handicapped lobby turned to the courts. The 1972 landmark decision, *Mills v. the Board of Education in the District of Columbia,* established the right of handicapped children to a free, publicly supported education "regardless of the degree of the child's mental, physical or emotional disability or impairment." Furthermore, no child could be excluded from "such publicly supported education on the basis of a claim of insufficient resources."[14] Similar court action followed in 27 other states.

Section 504 of the Rehabilitation Act of 1973 opened up further opportunities for court action by providing the handicapped constituency with a federal law defining the civil rights of handicapped people. Echoing the wording and the intent of Title VI of the 1964 Civil Rights Act, Section 504 "forbids any program or activity receiving Federal assistance from discriminating against any persons because of a handicapping condition." The ultimate goal, said legislators supporting the law, was "to bring about the full integration of handicapped individuals into all aspects of society."[15]

Concerns raised about the high costs of ensuring full participation of the handicapped and the impossibility of attaining this goal were brushed aside. The head of the Department of Health, Education and Welfare's Office for Civil Rights Technical Assistance called them "irrelevant." "Someone's rights do not depend upon someone else's ability to pay," a colleague added, "It is a matter of the right to participate in American society."[16]

The *sine qua non* of the lobby's efforts to achieve full integration of handicapped children into the regular school system was the enactment in 1975 of The Education for All Handicapped Children Act (P.L. 94-142). The law requires that every state and local school district afford every handicapped child (between the ages of three and twenty-one) within its jurisdiction a "free and appropriate public education," without regard to the parents' income or the state's or locality's ability to pay, in the "least restrictive environment." This means that wherever possible handicapped and nonhandicapped children must be placed in the same classroom—so-called mainstreaming—with supplemental instruction in separate classrooms for handicapped students.

---

[14]*Congressional Record,* Senate, June 18, 1975, p. 19485.
[15]*Congressional Record,* House, June 5, 1973, p. 18126.
[16]"Intergovernmentalizing the Classroom," *op. cit.,* p. 65.

The law establishes elaborate due process procedures that encourage parents to sue whenever they are dissatisfied with a teacher's or school's handling of their child. It opens up the child's records to parental inspection, thereby leading to the removal by school authorities of much of the information teachers need to give children an effective education. And it requires that an Individualized Education Plan (IEP) be written for every handicapped child. This has consumed valuable time, in some cases has supplanted standardized achievement testing, and has increased the cost of educating a handicapped child. Worse, by fragmenting the learning process, magnifying each fragment, and labeling any weakness as indicative of a handicap, the IEPs have justified the mislabeling of normal children.

One of the most costly and unreasonable requirements of P.L. 94-142 is that school districts pay for the related services accompanying mainstreaming efforts. These include eliminating architectural barriers (installing elevators in some cases), hiring specially trained personnel (such as psychologists, physical therapists, therapeutic recreation specialists, diagnostic personnel, and supervisors), catheterizing students, paying for psychotherapy, and subsidizing private school tuition for those children who cannot be taught in the public school.[17]

The Results

Most studies of The Education for All Handicapped Children Act have focused upon the ability of the state and local education agencies to pay for the Act's requirements. Their findings: states and localities are crippled by the excessive costs of educating handicapped children in the "least restrictive environment." Education Turnkey Systems, Inc., a Virginia-based evaluation firm released a report in 1981 describing the expenditures of "states and localities on special services to handicapped children as 'uncontrollable.'" One investigator found that 25 percent of one "state's local school transportation budget is spent on handicapped children who make up only three percent of the total school population."[18]

In response to such figures, some in the handicap lobby argue that the heavy costs associated with P.L. 94-142 are less than the cost of one alternative to the program—lifetime institutionalization. This is a strawman, because few handicaps require lifetime institutionaliza-

---

[17]Subpart B—State Annual Program Plans and Local Applications, P.L. 94-142, Education for All Handicapped Children Act.
[18]Angela Giordano Evans, "Legislative History, U.S. Senate Floor Consideration of S.6, Education for All Handicapped Children Act of 1975" (Washington, D.C.: The Library of Congress Congressional Research Service, August 29, 1975), p. 11.

tion. Moreover, many children now labeled handicapped and given expensive remedial treatment are mislabeled. Ignored completely, however, is the impact of P.L. 94-142 on the students—the normal and the mainstreamed handicapped—and on the regular school system.

Mislabeling

When P.L. 94-142 first became law, the term "learning disability" was not included in the definition of a handicap because Congress rightly feared it would lead to improper labeling. The U.S. Office of Education had estimated that the definition of "learning disabilities" (LD) was so vague that the bottom 25 percent of any class could be so labeled. Congress's fears have been justified since 1977, when regulations defining LD were added to the law. Between 1977 and 1983, the number of children labeled LD has increased 119 percent.[19] LD children now comprise some two-thirds of all children labeled handicapped.[20]

Leading experts in the field of special education estimate that 50 to 75 percent of all children labeled LD have been mislabeled. The probable reasons stem from strong professional incentives to mislabel. These include the simple fact that "finding" more LD children enables a school to receive more state and federal funds, to allow teachers to avoid teaching responsibilities to slow learners, to guarantee the jobs of special needs personnel, to justify the need for remediation programs in the regular school system, and to create a market for special classroom materials. As such, mislabeling fuels an industry that has grown beyond an honest need for its services.

Fragmentation of the Curriculum

The resource room model, created to provide pull-out, supplemental instruction for mainstreamed "handicapped" students, in too many schools has become a dumping ground for regular students having academic difficulties. In addition, it has contributed significantly to weakening the elementary and secondary school curricula, because of a general absence of instructional coordination and generalizability between it and the regular classroom, and the resulting fragmentation of the labeled child's instructional program. Generally, children are sent to the resource room during periods of academic instruction in subject area competencies in the regular

---

[19]*Education Times,* February 13, 1984, p. 6.
[20]Ravitch, *op. cit.,* p. 310.

classroom. Since what the children receive in the resource room is often of questionable value and application, it is quite possible that overall the labeled student loses much more than he gains.

Mainstreaming

Although P.L. 94-142 strongly encourages the integration of truly handicapped children into regular classrooms, general educators have had difficulty dealing effectively with these special needs children. This should come as no surprise to anyone who has observed classrooms for normal and special children. The normal schoolroom, whose primary purpose is group academic instruction, does not lend itself to serving handicapped children. The classes are too big; the teacher's time and attention must be divided among all the children; having to devote an inordinate amount of time to a few detracts from the whole.

Litigation

The due process provisions in P.L. 94-142 also have changed the nature of the parent-school relationship and caused resentment and distrust on both sides. This is because the due process approach takes the responsibility for the child from the parent and places it solely in the hands of the state. It changes the focus from one of a parent helping his child with the assistance of other agencies to one of litigation, where agencies are forced to do what in many instances the parent ought to do—without regard to the cost imposed on the community.

The Dilemma

Bitter opposition from the handicap lobby greets all proposals to reform the Education for All Handicapped Children Act. In 1982, the Reagan Administration proposed some much needed changes in the Act, including revising some of the present definitions, such as related services and time-line requirements for Individualized Education Plans (IEPs). It also sought to restrict the provisions for mainstreaming and free and appropriate education in the law. In addition, the proposed changes authorized local education agencies to consider how a handicapped child's behavior might disrupt nonhandicapped children before placing him in a regular classroom.

Administration officials failed to buttress these reasonable proposals with carefully organized grassroots support. Many school principals and school board members, for instance, would have welcomed a change in P.L. 94-142 regulations. But the Administration failed to consult with or mobilize them while the regulations were being drafted. The handicap lobby, on the other hand, was well prepared to defend its turf. After emotional hearings before Congress in 1982, Secretary of Education Terrel Bell withdrew the proposed regulations, and President Reagan announced that his Administration had abandoned its review of the law.

To date, the issues of what constitutes a proper education for handicapped children and whose primary responsibility it is remain insufficiently addressed.

Bilingual Education

A common language is the mortar binding people and communities into a nation. It is the hallmark of every great civilization. In Canada, the bitter battle over English and French threatens to divide the country politically. A similar danger to the U.S. cannot be ignored.

The Campaign

Prior to 1968, nearly every state forbade the use of any language other than English as the main language of classroom instruction.[21] In 1967, however, there were proposals in Washington to use "ethnicity as a basis for public policy."[22] Hispanic spokesmen and politicians claimed that Hispanic children had poor self-concepts, low self-esteem, low achievement levels, and poor attitudes toward school because the public school system failed to teach them their native language and culture.[23] If these children were taught and achieved greater competence in their native language, it was argued, they ultimately would be better able to make the transition to English. This argument prevailed, leading to the 1968 Bilingual Education Act.[24]

During the first years of the program, limited funds were given to local education agencies (LEAs), or to colleges working with LEAs, to develop "imaginative preschool and elementary and secondary school" demonstration programs.[25] No district was required to par-

---

[21] Angela Evans, "Bilingual Education: Federal Policy Issues," Issue Brief No. IB 83131 (Washington, D.C.: The Library of Congress, Congressional Research Service, Major Issue System, Updated May 17, 1984).
[22] Ravitch, *op. cit.*, p. 271.
[23] *Ibid.*
[24] Hugh Davis Graham, "The Transportation of Federal Policy: The Kennedy and Johnson Years" (Chapel Hill, North Carolina: U.N.C. Press, to be published).
[25] Mary T. Olguin, "Elementary and Secondary Education Act as Amended Through 1967" (Washington, D.C.: Library of Congress, Legislative Reference Service, February 28, 1969).

ticipate in the experiment, and there was no strict definition of bilingual education. By 1970, however, the Office for Civil Rights in the Department of Health, Education, and Welfare was "advising" school districts with over 5 percent National-Origin-Minority-Group children to "open" their instructional program to limited-English-speaking-ability students.[26]

The 1974 Supreme Court decision, *Lau v. Nichols,* mandated the creation of special language programs and paved the way for deep congressional involvement in bilingual education. Using civil rights arguments, the Court declared that English-language-deficient children in English classes had been denied an equal educational opportunity under Title VI of the 1964 Civil Rights Act. Although no prescription was given, the Court suggested teaching English to the students and instructing them in their native tongue.[27]

In response to this, Congress replaced the original Title VII provisions with a new Bilingual Education Act. It stated that any school receiving federal funds would be required to provide "appropriate" services to language minority students.[28] An Office of Bilingual Education was created in the U.S. Office of Education.

The Results

The most troubling provision of the new Act allowed limited (up to 40 percent) voluntary enrollment in bilingual classes of children whose primary language was English. This was supposedly "to foster appreciation of the cultural heritage of limited-English-speaking-ability children." The result of this was not to bring limited-English-speaking-ability children into the American culture; rather, it was to lock them into an environment that would remain a minority within American society and to draw into this minority environment the children of the main culture.

The Lau Remedies of 1975, drafted by the U.S. Office of Education, reinforced this interpretation. In an effort to mandate native language instruction and bicultural education under the respectable guise of providing federal guidelines for the *Lau v. Nichols* Supreme Court decision, the Lau Remedies actually prohibited English-as-a-Second-Language instruction. On the other hand, they endorsed pure native language instruction as an acceptable alternative to instruction in English. They then added that students should be taught about their

---

[26]Ravitch, *op. cit.,* p. 274.
[27]*Lau v. Nichols,* 414 .S. 563 (1974).
[28]Bilingual Education Act of 1974 (P.L. 93-308).

native culture—an issue never mentioned by the Supreme Court.[29] Although objections resulted in revoking the prohibition of English-as-a-Second-Language by the Office for Civil Rights, districts not offering "bilingual" instruction were required to prove their programs were as effective as those which did.

This was difficult for them to do. Competent studies assessing the effectiveness of bilingual education are hard to find. Many studies either have been aborted or ignored.[30] Many of those that do exist paint a dismal picture of bilingual education. A 1974 survey of Title VII projects by the National Education Task Force de la Raza, for instance, reported that up to 87 percent of the bilingual programs merely reinforced the minority language, rather than providing a transition to a society based on English.[31] And the comprehensive study of Title VII—by the American Institutes for Research,[32] under contract to the U.S. Office of Education—found that Title VII programs were generally ineffective in improving English language competency and that two-thirds of the students in Title VII programs in 1976 in grades two through six actually had an adequate command of English. Indeed, of Title VII project directors, 86 percent were reported to have a policy of keeping students in such classes after they could learn in English.[33]

The bilingual lobby has attacked these results. By so doing, it makes clear that its purpose for bilingual education is to promote a separate culture within the U.S.

In 1978, Congress greatly expanded the number of eligible participants by changing the definition from limited-English-speaking-ability to limited-English-proficient (LEP). This definition typically has been interpreted to mean that exposure to a second language (e.g., the child's parents speak a foreign tongue but the child speaks English) is reason enough to place the child in a bilingual education class. The 1978 measures also have been interpreted to mean that a child's low achievement indicates a need for bilingual education. Yet Hispanic students have not been found to do better in school as a result of bilingual education. The low academic achievement and the high drop-out rate among this population is legion.

---

[29]Evans, *op. cit.,* 1984.

[30]Robert Rossier and Martin Wooster, "Hysteria with Footnotes" (Washington, D.C.: LEARN, Inc., 1984).

[31]Noel Epstein, "Bilingual Education in the U.S.: The 'Either/Or' Mistake," Paper delivered at the University of Chicago, Center for Policy Studies Conference, 1978, p. 99.

[32]Angela Evans, "Overview of the Federal Bilingual Education Programs and Participants" (Washington, D.C.: Library of Congress, Congressional Research Service, November 1978).

[33]Evans, *op. cit.,* 1984, p. 2.

The 1978 Education Amendments reiterated that any bilingual instruction program may consist of up to 40 percent English-speaking children who do not fit the federal LEP definition—this time to "prevent segregation of children on the basis of national origin [and] . . . . to assist children of limited English proficiency to improve their English language skills."[34]

In August 1980, then Secretary of Education Shirley Hufstedler issued proposed Lau regulations to replace the Lau Remedies. These were in essence civil rights directives mandating the establishment of a separate sub-society in the public schools. Denial of access to bilingual education programs to any federally defined limited-English-proficient (LEP) student was to be forbidden. Worse, public schools were required to teach LEP children in their native language (that is, in any one of 87 foreign tongues). Up to 100 percent of the classes, moreover, could be composed of English-speaking children.[35] A widespread revolt in the education community led incoming Secretary of Education Terrel Bell to revoke the Lau regulations on February 2, 1982,[36] although it often seems that the regulations still guide Department actions.

Buttressed by reports recommending alternative instructional methods and state and local control,[37] the Reagan Administration made attempts to define bilingual education at the federal level by proposing a new act, "The Bilingual Education Improvement Act," which prohibited restrictions on the kind of instructional methods to be used by school districts.[38] Although the measure had bipartisan support, an apparent unwillingness to jeopardize the Hispanic vote led the Administration to retreat from its own bill. A compromise bill, which authorized only 10 percent of its funding for alternative instruction, was adopted and signed into law October 19, 1984, ensuring the status quo in bilingual education for at least another four years.

The experience of the past two decades should have taught the nation that it must return to the common understanding and assumption that "the standard tongue is the appropriate device for individual and national life in a modern civilization."[39] English must prevail as the primary language of instruction in America's schools.

---

[34]Bilingual Education Act of 1978, Section 703.
[35]Evans, *op. cit.*, 1984.
[36]*Ibid.*
[37]Evans, *op. cit.*, 1984.
[38]*Ibid.*
[39]Jacques Barzun, "Language and Life—Talk by J. Barzun," Discussion Series, U.S. English (Washington, D.C., 1983).

The Women's Educational Equity Act

No door of opportunity should be closed to anyone capable of opening it. On the other hand, none should be opened artificially for anyone who will not or cannot enter it on his or her own. This ensures the proper channeling of human resources into areas of greatest compatibility and productivity.

Seeking to redefine nature to conform to dogma, radical feminists have sought to destroy this process and ignore real differences between individuals by demanding that the national government require absolute parity between the sexes in all federal programs, repudiate any findings of differences as "sexist," and financially penalize the institution that acts upon them. In their determination to separate cause from effect, radical feminists demand an end to all "discrimination" against women by ignoring even obvious physical factors. These efforts are doubly damaging: they put women in programs where they do not belong, and they keep men and women alike out of programs where they do belong.

The Campaign

During the 1960s, organizations such as the National Organization for Women (NOW) and the Women's Equity Action League (WEAL) were formed to use civil rights arguments to establish federal laws prohibiting discrimination on the basis of sex and to challenge "sex discrimination" by judicial means in education and industry. The major goals were to place women in fields traditionally considered masculine and to alter society's understanding of gender roles.

Social causation[40] was the main theory informing the creation and actions of these feminist organizations. According to its reasoning, sexual differences are primarily the result of social conditioning rather than innately determined; since social conditions shape man's nature and since man creates social conditions, it is reasoned, "inequalities" between the sexes are attributable to social discrimination and can be righted through social action.

The radical feminists and their ideology won passage of Title IX of the Higher Education Act of 1972. This civil rights statute states that "no person in the United States shall, on the basis of sex, be excluded from participation in, be denied the benefits of, or be subject to discrimination under any education program or activity receiving

---

[40]Frank S. Zepezauer, "Threading Through the Feminist Minefield," *Phi Delta Kappan,* December 1981, pp. 268-272.

federal financial assistance." Authored by Congresswoman Edith Green (D-OR), Title IX was considered relatively unimportant by education groups and Congress. This indifference left policy makers at the Department of Health, Education, and Welfare free to apply the statute as they pleased.[41] Following Title IX's passage, the Office for Civil Rights in the Office of Education informed universities that they could not allocate "disproportionate" sums to male athletics; neither could they award more athletic scholarships to male students than to female students. In a major assault on America's traditional practice of protecting young people, college dormitories were even forbidden to enforce parietal rules for girls' and boys' residences.[42]

In 1973 the Office for Civil Rights demanded that schools identify any classes with 80 percent or more students from one sex. Female college faculty members then began to file suits over what they claimed was unequal pay—a trend that has since spread to many areas of employment.[43]

Determined to change the nation's attitude toward gender, the radical feminists drafted a proposal in 1971 calling for federal funding of efforts to eliminate what they felt to be sex role stereotyping. Two years later Representative Patsy Mink (D-HA) introduced the Women's Educational Equity Act (WEEA), and helped incorporate it into the 1974 Education Amendments via the catch-all Education Projects Act. Explaining the low profile used to obtain passage, Congresswoman Mink declared, "If it had to be hidden to get enacted, so be it. So we hid it."[44]

---

[41]"Intergovernmentalizing the Classroom," *op. cit.,* p. 63-64.

[42]Ravitch, *op. cit.,* p. 297.

[43]It has long been the contention of female activists that the white male dominated social structure has frozen women out of higher paying positions and has paid them less once they have fought their way into them. Yet data indicate that inequality in pay and status is due primarily to voluntary choices by women (to have children during the critical years of career advancement, for example) and to motivational differences between the sexes. In the early 1980s, the XYZ Company (a Fortune 500 Company) was accused of discriminating against women because it had male-female employment imbalances in managerial positions. A study of the alleged discriminatory practices, however, showed that the firm's comparatively low proportion of women promotees was the result of behavioral and attitudinal differences between male and female clerks and not the result of discrimination: the same opportunities had been offered to both sexes, but men had sought promotions more often than women. In addition, women have been found to be more reluctant than men to move to secure a promotion. Thus, the lower pay/status of working women may well be the by-product of free choice. Carol Hoffman and John S. Reed, "Sex Discrimination?—The XYZ Affair," *Public Interest,* Winter 1981, pp. 21-39.

[44]Mary Ann Millsap and Leslie Wolfe, "A Feminist Perspective in Law and Practice: The Women's Educational Equity Act," Reported in Rosemary Thomson's "History of the Women's Educational Equity Act (WEEA)," Preliminary Draft Notes (Washington, D.C.: Women's Educational Equity Council, 1982).

WEEA awards grants and contracts to public and private nonprofit agencies and individuals to overhaul textbooks, curricula, and other educational materials to reflect a "nonsexist" world view—in effect, to reflect the radical feminist world view. It provides funding for preservice and inservice training; guidance and counseling (including the development of "nondiscriminatory tests"); and research, development, and educational activities to advance what the radicals call "educational equity."

This was done despite the total lack of evidence that girls had been affected adversely by such things as traditional textbooks. Girls consistently have outperformed boys in school and, particularly in the elementary grades, are better balanced, behaved, and appear to have a higher self-esteem.[45] By the middle grades boys generally begin to outstrip the girls in mathematical reasoning ability—a superiority they retain throughout their lives. The available evidence suggests that this difference between the sexes in mathematical reasoning, however, is not the result of social engineering or sexual discrimination, but rather of innate differences between the sexes.

An extensive study by Johns Hopkins University researchers confirms this. Over 40,000 seventh graders were given the Scholastic Aptitude Test (consisting of verbal and mathematical sections). Results showed a large difference between the sexes in mathematical reasoning by age thirteen—a difference that was greatest at the upper end of the distribution.[46] (Among the students scoring at or above 700, boys outnumbered girls by 13 to 1.) The stunning difference in performance could not be attributed to differences in instruction, the researchers noted, since none of the participating students had received formal instruction from algebra onward, and both sexes had received similar formal mathematics training. Differences in social conditions for boys and girls were not substantial enough, the study found, to account for the wide disparity in performance: marked differences in boys' and girls' interests were not found.[47]

In spite of evidence and common sense, the radical feminists relentlessly pursued their agenda and pushed for a new WEEA in 1977. The goal was to bring it out of hiding and to establish it as a separate categorical program within the Elementary and Secondary Education Act (ESEA). They succeeded the following year with the 1978 Education Amendments. WEEA was incorporated into the ESEA as a separate categorical program, with authorizations for each

---

[45]Ravitch, *op. cit.*
[46]"Sex Differences in Mathematical Reasoning Ability," *Science,* December 2, 1983, p. 1029.
[47]*Ibid.*

of fiscal years 1980-1983 set at $80 million (up from the $30 million authorized by the former WEEA).[48]

The purpose of this new Act was to provide agencies with financial assistance to meet the requirements of Title IX. Activities to promote "sex equity" were given funding priority. And true to form for any campaign wishing to expand the federal role, a separate office was created within the Office of Education—the Women's Educational Equity Act Program, complete with a Director and staff.

The Results

The radical feminist agenda had obtained a solid foothold in American society. At the local level, radicals relentlessly pursued the "desexing" of textbooks and children's books. Textbook companies responded, and students have been subjected to the feminist world view ever since: through illustrations of women mining engineers, for example, and men happily tending the baby, wearing an apron, and stirring a pot during the day. The National Organization for Women's Legal Defense and Education Fund was awarded a federal grant for Project PEER, which developed and disseminated to local activists a manual detailing strategies for changing a school's program, policy, or practice "that channels girls in one direction and boys in another."[49] Some radical feminist groups even received federal funding to promote their destructive sex ideology in the nation's public school classrooms.

In higher education, Title IX, despite its program specific wording, came to be enforced on an institution wide basis. Moreover, the regulations attached to Title IX were based on an "effects" definition of discrimination—that is, a practice is considered discriminatory if it has the effect, not necessarily the intent, of excluding a disproportionate number of legally protected groups. Thus, if a disproportionately small number of female academics are represented in the highest echelons of university life, it is to be considered the result of sex discrimination. As a result, many institutions of higher education were plunged, during the 1970s, into costly law suits and court settlements.[50]

---

[48]Wayne Riddle, Angela Evans, Bob Lyke, and Mark Wolfe, "Summary of the Education Amendments of 1978, Public Law 95-561" (Washington, D.C.: The Library of Congress Congressional Research Service, January 17, 1979).

[49]Copies available from PEER, Ninth Floor, 1413 K Street, N.W., Washington, D.C. 20005.

[50]Ravitch, *op. cit.*

The Reagan Administration, which repeatedly has sought to eliminate WEEA's funds, tried to fold the Act into the Chapter 2 Block Grant of the 1981 Omnibus Budget Reconciliation Act. Yet WEEA was retained as a separate categorical program under the Secretary of Education's Discretionary Fund. Appropriations, however, were cut to $6 million for fiscal years 1982-1984. Nevertheless, the kind of federal grants awarded by WEEA included $25,000 to "assist women in overcoming the most significant barrier [to] employment as firefighters:. . . . passing the physical ability test," through posters, a manual, and a videotape. Another $202,902 grant went to "minimize the negative consequences of early pregnancy." And a $24,139 grant was "to assist learning disabled women in adjusting to a male-oriented environment."[51]

In contradiction of Reagan's stated policies, the White House in 1984 was pressured by Secretary Bell and the education lobby to approve legislation extending WEEA for another five years and increasing its funding to $20 million by FY 1989.

Conclusion

The record shows that, when control of education is placed in federal hands, it is not controlled by "the people," but by small yet powerful lobbies motivated by self-interest or dogma. When centralized in this way, it is beyond the control of the parents and local communities it is designed to serve. It becomes impervious to feedback. Furthermore, once established, such programs seem to increase exponentially, even when authoritative studies question their effectiveness. Worst of all, Congress seems unable to resist the pressure from dogmatic groups and to act responsibly in the interest of the nation.

The failures of education since the instatement of President Johnson's Great Society programs are due in large part to centralized, special interest control at the federal level. It behooves the American people, Congress, and the education establishment to learn from these failures and to start now to reduce the federal presence in America's unique system of schooling for its youth.

---

[51]Funded September 1983.

4

Higher Education Today

by
Philip F. Lawler

An innocent browser, picking up at random a few copies of the weekly *Chronicle of Higher Education,* might well be confused. The most widely read publication covering American university life does not devote much attention to the study of history, or literature, or chemistry. The *Chronicle*'s headlines refer instead to affirmative action programs, BEOG grants, and Title IX implementation. The *Chronicle of Higher Education* has become a newspaper about the federal government.

Nor do the stories carried in the *Chronicle* relate directly to the aims of academic instruction. Only rarely do the articles detail how a federal government program can help bring concrete results in the classroom. Rather, they describe the complex administrative procedures through which a university can attract government support, implement the programs involved, and avoid conflicts with the myriad government regulations that come along with the support.

Quite often, the programs nourished by government funds are not regular aspects of university life; they spring into being because federal grants make them possible. On other occasions, government aid to an ongoing program changes the nature of that program. And regardless of the programs themselves, the ancillary costs of government regulation fundamentally change the behavior of the university. This raises the key question of whether the federal government can help—or does it hurt—the university in the pursuit of its ultimate goals.

The Goals of Higher Learning

The purpose of higher education, as traditionally understood, is the pursuit of truth. The liberal arts—"the arts of free men"—are not vocational training aids, but tools for the development of a student's critical faculties. Ideally, an institution of higher education is where students and faculty can set themselves apart from the bustle of everyday affairs and ponder the more enduring, profound questions of philosophical discourse. Soon enough, most liberal arts students will be absorbed into the maelstrom of career activities. But for these few years, as they enter into adulthood, they are allowed the opportunity to learn from great thinkers of every age, so that later they will be able to put contemporary events into a broader, more far-sighted perspective.

Anyone who pauses to reflect on that traditional understanding of university life cannot fail to notice the difference between the abstract, quiet atmosphere of the university and the practical, noisy world of democratic politics. Particularly in a democracy, political issues are decided not by reference to philosophical truths, but by a majority vote. A university can never be satisfied in its quest for knowledge; a democracy must be satisfied with a rough-and-ready consensus to support a government program. Democratic politics and liberal education make strange bedfellows.

In individual cases, there might be opportunities for partnership between university and government. Government scholarships might help worthy students, and university scientists might fulfill the research needs of particular government programs. But even such limited partnerships pose problems for the university.

Any university that today accepts support from the federal government must be aware that it comes with strings attached. To accept federal money is to accept federal control. In fact, the proposed so-called Civil Rights Act of 1984, which failed to pass in Congress, would have broadened the scope of federal regulation enormously. The Act, intended to "clarify congressional intent" as to the applicability of federal regulations, was designed to extend the government's authority to cover any program at any school that received any federal assistance. Under the terms of this legislation, a school would have been classified as a recipient of federal funds if any individual student were to accept government-subsidized loans. The range of government regulations details the conduct of university life and colors the school's perception of its own ultimate goals. To accept government aid, then, might mean to accept Uncle Sam's idea of the purpose of higher education.

Just how much control can the federal government exert over an independent university that accepts its aid? That question has provoked an intense legal controversy over the past decade. In a series of intriguing court battles, small private schools have argued that, since they accept no direct federal grants, they should be free from government regulation. But many, in turn, have argued that there has been federal aid to a college if even one undergraduate student takes advantage of government-subsidized student loans to pay tuition. In the most recent landmark suit, the case of *Grove City College*,[1] the

---

[1] See *Newsweek*, March 12, 1984, p. 86, or *Time*, March 12, 1984, p. 119.

U.S. Supreme Court accepted the latter interpretation of that crucial question. However, the Court ruled—somewhat implausibly—that government regulations could be enforced only in the particular programs directly subsidized by government funds. The argument over that issue undoubtedly will continue until a more complete set of legal precedents emerges.

Federal intervention is not a danger to private schools alone. State-supported schools are even more vulnerable, since they rely even more heavily on federal aid. The onus of being found in "noncompliance" with federal rules weighs heavily on a state Board of Regents; state systems probably could not survive without federal grants, and the negative publicity that accompanies a federal reprimand saps a state's will to guide its own school system independently. The North Carolina university system, in particular, has been forced to implement a series of institutional contortions (most recently, moving a dental school onto the campus of a predominantly black college to change the racial mix on that campus) to stave off federal reprimands. If private schools are in danger of losing a measure of their autonomy, state university systems are in danger of losing their distinctiveness altogether and becoming simply local branches of a federal higher education network.

When the federal government intervenes on campus, its purpose is not to improve the quality of teaching or raise the academic standards of particular disciplines. In each of the landmark battles over government control, the issue at stake has been federal enforcement of affirmative action guidelines in a university— federal efforts to guarantee treatment of minorities (under the aegis of Title VI of the 1964 Civil Rights Act) or women (via Title IX of the 1972 Education Amendments). How these issues are related to the pursuit of truth, the real purpose of higher education, is unclear.

New Roles for Academe

Until the end of World War II, the federal government had only a minimal involvement in the process of higher education. Colleges still accommodated only a small portion of the students who graduated from secondary schools. When the troops came home from the war, however, Congress demanded that they be offered the best opportunities society could provide. A college education was considered small payment for the job the soldiers had done, and the GI Bill allowed an enormous number of veterans to enroll in the nation's universities. For the first time, Washington used the universities for a political end.

This was just the beginning of a series of changes that the federal government would force on academe. The GI Bill made college education a realistic goal for thousands of Americans; the liberal arts colleges would never be elite preserves again. And for the mature GI, a college degree was not a luxury; it was a ticket to career opportunities. University enrollment soared for a generation. In 1950, American universities granted 433,734 bachelor's degrees and 6,420 doctorates. By 1980, those figures had climbed to 1,017,250 bachelor's degrees (an increase of 235 percent) and 32,750 doctorates (an increase of 510 percent).[2] By the time the original beneficiaries of the GI Bill had raised college-age children, higher education was the rule rather than the exception. Indeed, a college degree became a necessity for anyone contemplating a professional career. More and more, a college education was seen as an investment in "human capital," a means of increasing the student's market value.

From Washington's perspective, the marketplace value of higher education always has overshadowed the more abstract values of the liberal arts ideal. As federal spending on social programs grew, politicians and academics alike found new possibilities for partnership between an active government and a willing academy. During the dizzying period of growth that swept American universities in the 1960s, Clark Kerr—then President of the University of California and one of the most influential figures in the educational establishment—coined the term "multiversity" to describe higher education's new role.[3] The multiversity would serve any number of different functions simultaneously. It would be all things to all men.

The multiversity, as Kerr explained it, would be a research facility serving purely scientific, technical, corporate, and government interests. It would be a think tank producing new solutions to social problems. It would be a melting pot, introducing students across cultural gaps. It would be a social service provider, helping educate children in the slums nearby. In a word, the university would serve the democracy.

In the enthusiasm to fulfill the promise of the multiversity, American universities stampeded into a wild expansion in all manner of different pursuits. Whole new faculties sprang up within the universities, and the number of course offerings rose exponentially. In the 1950s, the catalogues of course offerings at Harvard and Princeton hovered around 50 pages. Today, these catalogues run over 500 pages.

By the end of the 1960s, university life was irreversibly changed. Students pursued an infinite variety of programs, with the help of ever

---

[2]*American Colleges and Universities,* 12th Edition, edited by the American Council on Education (New York, 1983), p. 8.
[3]See Clark Kerr, *The Uses of the University* (Cambridge, Massachusetts: Harvard University Press, 1963).

increasing government financial aid. Curricular requirements changed dramatically, enabling students to design their own course of studies. Independent work had become commonplace, as had programs awarding credit for work experience. Above all, universities had left behind the vision of ivory tower detachment to permit abstract philosophical studies. The university was a means to an end—whether that end was a higher salary for an individual student, or a research product for a major corporation, or a new campaign platform for a political party.

Furthermore, the life of the university was no longer seen as an end in itself. In 1972, U.S. Commissioner of Education (of the U.S. Office of Education) Terrel Bell commented, "I feel that the college that devotes itself totally and unequivocally to the liberal arts is just kidding itself."[4] The man who uttered those words became Ronald Reagan's first Secretary of Education.

In this new perception of the university, the traditional liberal arts were overtaken by the younger, more glamorous sciences. The multiversity, with its eye on usefulness, gave short shrift to the less marketable aspects of higher learning.

Even while the university enjoyed the fruits of its growth, some analysts wondered whether such an increasingly disparate range of interests could be accommodated by one fragile institution. Writing in 1971, Columbia University's Professor Emeritus Robert Nisbet worried about the future of the university:

> I refer to ... the university's role as higher capitalist, chief of the research establishment, superhumanitarian, benign therapist, adjunct government, and loyal opposition. Each of these is doubtless a worthy role in society. What passes imagination, however, is any conception of their being harnessed together in a single institution that continues to insist upon its aristocratic or priestly virtue in the cause of dispassionate reason.[5]

Losing Sight of the Goal

What changes has this new understanding of academic life wrought in the university? Nothing illustrates the impact of political influence more dramatically than the results of affirmative action programs.

Twenty years after President Lyndon Johnson introduced the

---

[4] Philip Lawler, "A Question of Educatonal Freedom," Special issue of *Prospect,* January 1977, p. 18.
[5] Robert Nisbet, *The Degradation of the Academic Dogma* (New York: Basic Books, 1971), Introduction.

concept, affirmative action is virtually enshrined in American universities. In an effort to help minority groups raise their socioeconomic status, universities set up special recruiting drives, special admissions standards, and often even special remedial courses to accommodate these favored groups. The Reagan Administration's National Commission on Excellence in Education reported that "Between 1975 and 1980, remedial mathematics courses in public 4-year colleges increased by 72% and now constitute one-quarter of all mathematics courses taught in those institutions."[6]

The inner logic of the program is political, not academic; the ultimate goal is to provide cadres of educated young people from the designated groups, who can then act as leaders within their own ethnic communities. In 1974, the Urban League's Vernon Jordan wrote that "So long as blacks constitute a smaller proportion of college graduates and holders of advanced degrees, they will necessarily constitute a smaller proportion of college faculty members."[7] By the same token, Jordan continued, blacks (and other minorities) will achieve equal opportunity in American society only when they matriculate in numbers reflecting their percentage of the overall population. Affirmative action in higher education, in short, is believed by many to be a vital step toward arranging American society equitably. The logic of affirmative action leaves one crucial question unanswered. Why should the university be designated to remedy social inequalities?

Affirmative action programs in higher education have created a host of new problems, menacing the health of the academic community. Many minority students would have qualified for admission (and minority professors, for tenure) without special preference. For them, affirmative action means devaluation of their achievement. On the other hand, other minority students come to school unprepared for academic competition and become discouraged or alienated by the pressure. Even the most resilient minority scholars feel the additional pressure of their special status; they come to the campus not merely as individual students but as specially designated standard-bearers for their communities. In 1972, when he learned that Swarthmore College was actively seeking a black economist, Thomas Sowell—himself a black who is an eminent economist—wrote to the department chairman, pointing out that "Your approach tends to make the job unattractive to anyone who regards himself as a scholar or a man, and thereby throws it open to opportunists."[8]

---

[6] *A Nation at Risk,* a report by the National Commission on Excellence in Education (Washington, D.C.: Government Printing Office, 1983), p. 9.

[7] Vernon Jordan, "Blacks and Higher Education—Some Reflections," *Daedalus,* Winter 1975.

[8] Letter of Professor Frank C. Pierson, dated September 18, 1972; quoted in George C. Roche, *The Balancing Act* (LaSalle, Illinois: Open Court, 1974), p. 41.

Affirmative action also offends a fundamental ideal of academic life. In the world of scholarship, a professor's family background counts for nothing; his ideas and his ability to defend them are all that matter. The notion of affirmative action subverts this ideal, leading the school to set quotas for the admission of minority students and the appointment of minority teachers to the faculty. Naturally, this provokes intense resentment among the groups hurt by reverse discrimination; on many U.S. campuses, the advent of affirmative action programs has increased racial tension.

In the rush to root out social inequalities, federal regulators have asked the universities to prohibit discrimination on the basis of race, sex, linguistic background, and physical or emotional handicap. Yet a university is inherently discriminating; it discriminates against stupidity and teaches students to discriminate against mediocrity in intellectual pursuits. To ask a university to stop discriminating is tantamount to prohibiting serious scholarship. The key question— and one which the universities should answer for themselves—is what are the legitimate grounds for discrimination in academic life?

Academic freedom, too, has suffered from the politicization of the academy. Traditionally understood, academic freedom is a special privilege granted to scholars in their pursuit of truth; it is society's recognition of the scholar's right to decide how to pursue research and how to express his or her findings. But in a politicized university, the concept of academic freedom is drastically redefined. The First Amendment still applies, to be sure. But today when scholars engage in controversial research or speak on controversial subjects, or when they defend academic privilege against government encroachment, academic freedom seems to afford very little protection.

During and after the campus upheavals of the Vietnam War era, the greatest threat to academic freedom came from radical students who routinely disrupted lectures, intimidating speakers with whom they did not agree. At the height of of the crisis, Harvard's James Q. Wilson lamented: "The list of subjects that cannot be discussed in a free and open forum has grown steadily, and now includes the war in Vietnam, public policy toward urban ghettos, the relationship between intelligence and heredity, and the role of American corporations in certain overseas regimes."[9] Even today, each spring brings stories of several speakers who have been shouted down at—or dissuaded from attending—university commencements.

Two recent examples come to mind. At the University of Georgia, an English professor was cited for contempt of court in 1980 because he refused to reveal how he had voted when a female professor was

---

[9]James Q. Wilson, "Liberalism Versus Liberal Education," *Commentary*, June 1972, p. 51.

proposed for tenure in his department.[10] Ordinarily a tenure decision is regarded as sacrosanct, with the professors who vote answerable to no one outside their own departments. But no professional organization recognized the threat to academic freedom in the Georgia case; the unfortunate professor faced his sentence alone.

One year later, a Stanford anthropologist was denied tenure after he published a highly controversial description of government sterilization programs in mainland China.[11] While the university refused to comment on the reasons for the negative decision, most observers believed (and the professor's Stanford colleagues admitted) that the controversy his research generated had ruined his changes for promotion. Apparently, the professor's critics felt that his harsh depiction of the Beijing government would impair academic relations between the two countries. By this logic, it would have been better to soft-pedal the professor's findings for diplomatic reasons. No one denied that his research was valid, but—in unambiguous contradiction of the spirit of academic freedom—his report was unwelcome.

The belief that federal involvement corrupts the purity of higher education is not held only by ivory tower philosophers. Nearly a decade ago, the publisher of *Scientific American,* Gerard Piel, made the same complaint:

> If the universities are now to restore their legitimacy, they must recover their innocence. The time has come to bring their federal period to a close.... In the innocent ideal, to elicit the thirst and capacity for rational inquiry is the aim of teaching, and the learning of the student follows in the tract of the teacher's inquiry. If some "service is owed," in addition, to the community, it is the community as it ought to be and not as it stands today. The university is the supremely normative institution of contemporary secular society. It cannot accept as given the purposes and values of other interests and institutions. Its resources are not for hire.[12]

Pitfalls of Federal Aid

Before federal aid to higher education became firmly established as a way of academic life, some observers recognized the potential costs of government largesse. In his 1953 testimony in the *A. P. Smith* court case, Princeton's President Harold Dodds remarked:

---

[10]*People,* September 20, 1980, pp. 37-38. Surely the fact that *People* provided the most extensive coverage of the controversy says something about the attitude of more "serious" journals toward troublesome cases involving academic freedom.

[11]"Trouble for a China Hand," *Newsweek,* November 2, 1981, p. 113.

[12]Gerard Piel, "Public Support for Autonomous Universities," *Daedalus,* Winter 1975, p. 151.

> There are educators that dream of a day of expansive federal grants-in-aid to both public state-supported and private institutions, and that this aid is to be divorced from all political control or accountability whatsoever. This dream I conceive to be both vain and immoral. It is vain because it will never be realized, for he who pays the piper calls the tune. It is immoral, because it is the duty of the governmental authority which raises taxes and spends the taxpayers's money to see that it is used in accordance with the will of the legislature.... Thus, both as a practical matter and as an ethical matter, the tax-sustained university will always be, and should always be, subject to political control.[13]

This statement was made at a time when federal aid to higher education was infinitesimal. When larger grants became available, the lure of government money overweighed the warnings of such educators as Dodds. In the span of a few decades, even the most securely endowed private universities came to depend on federal grants for a sizable portion of their operating budgets. In the late 1970s, Dodds's own Princeton looked to Washington for 40 percent of its annual support,[14] and other schools were even more dependent. By 1976, President William McGill of venerable Columbia University confessed that his institution was "only trivially different in this respect from the University of Michigan."[15]

Every school has sources of income outside the federal government: students' tuition and fees; gifts from alumni, foundations, and corporations; endowment and investment income all add to the coffers. But except for the most fortunate universities, these other income sources are dwarfed by the sums coming from Washington. In fact, in 1976 the editors of *Change* magazine estimated that American colleges spend more money on federal paperwork than they receive from all voluntary contributions.[16] A university might serve a wide ranging clientele, but the federal government is the one client that the university cannot afford to alienate.

Naturally, like other institutions facing their most powerful clients, the universities have taken great pains to oblige their government benefactors. The evidence is most obvious—and the damage to academic independence most severe—in the implementation of federal affirmative action programs, as set out by the Office for Civil Rights at the Department of Education.

To run afoul of the affirmative action guidelines, a university need not discriminate against minority students; failure to provide complete proof of compliance with the federal guidelines can be enough to

---

[13] *A. P. Smith Manufacturing Company vs. Barlow*, New Jersey, 1953.
[14] Lawler, *op. cit.*
[15] *Ibid.*
[16] Jerome M. Zigler, "Would State Control of Federal Education Dollars Be More or Less Desirable?" *Change*, October 1976, pp. 50-51.

cut off the flow of government funds. And even if the school passes the first federal test successfully, it is only a matter of time before the government requires another set of statistics, another master plan, and another assurance that affirmative action is being fully enforced. In 1972, Columbia University reported that its full Affirmative Action Program was a 316-page document, weighing some 3.5 pounds.[17] Since that time, Columbia will have revised its plan to take into consideration the serial reinterpretations of the 1964 Civil Rights Act, the 1972 Education Amendments, and a host of Executive Orders.

Thomas Sowell asks:

> Why is affirmative action so ineffective, despite the furor it arouses? Simply because its shotgun approach hits the just and the unjust alike. For example, the University of Michigan had to spend $35,000 just to collect statistics for affirmative action. For all practical purposes, that is the same as being assessed a $35,000 fine without either a charge or proof of anything.[18]

But the University of Michigan would much rather pay $35,000—quietly—than risk the hundreds of thousands of dollars in grants that flow into Ann Arbor from federal programs.

Schools not only set quotas for the admission of minority students, but also devise master plans for affirmative action in the appointment of faculty members. To fill those quotas, many universities also launch costly recruiting campaigns to locate qualified applicants. (Sometimes a recruiter must scour the countryside to find any applicants at all in a particular category, such as women engineering students.) Race, sex, and national origin become major determinants of a candidate's chances for admission to the student body or the faculty.

In the life of a university, no decisions are more important than those on faculty appointments. Traditionally, a professor's credentials are appraised by his peers. Thus the decisions on hiring, promotion, and granting tenure have been left in the hands of the various departments within the faculty. But with the advent of affirmative action master plans, the decisions of the department faculties have been subject to an effective veto by a federal bureaucrat, who may have no academic credentials whatsoever.

A few brave schools have bucked the trend and resisted the government's efforts to dictate academic policies. But the most

---

[17]George C. Roche, *op. cit.*, p. 1.
[18]Thomas Sowell, "A Black Conservative Dissents," *New York Times Magazine*, August 8, 1975, p. 156.

notable exponents of academic independence have been very small, private colleges: Hillsdale in Michigan, Rockford in Illinois, Grove City in Pennsylvania, and a handful of others. Ivy League universities have been silent, perhaps out of fear that backing their smaller counterparts might imperil their own beneficial relationship with government bureaucrats.

Government interference in academic life is not confined to admissions and faculty appointments. The scale of federal involvement in research also threatens the free scope of scientific inquiry. Here, too, the danger was recognized a generation ago. In a speech just before leaving the White House (which introduced the term "military-industrial complex" into the public lexicon), Dwight Eisenhower warned, "The prospect of domination of the nation's scholars by federal government, project allocation, and the power of money is ever present, and gravely to be regarded."[19]

Since Sputnik, and despite Eisenhower's warning, Uncle Sam has poured billions of dollars into campus research projects: on defense, agricultural productivity, fusion power, and a host of other topics, worthy and unworthy. The competition for these research grants has become highly politicized and frighteningly expensive. Major universities send their top administrators to Washington frequently, and many schools employ lobbyists on Capitol Hill to press their cases for federal grants. But the costs of establishing an institutional presence in Washington pale before the costs of maintaining a competitive research team.

A university seeking federal research grants in arcane scientific fields often must undertake considerable expense simply to demonstrate its capacity to handle the task. The risks to the university's finances, and to its academic idealism, are multiple. A major piece of equipment might be installed on campus—a cyclotron, for instance. Even if the expense can not be justified on its own merits, the lure and prestige of government grantsmanship might overcome ordinary prudence. And even if another school in the same town already had the necessary equipment (perhaps especially if another school had the equipment), administrators might regard winning a major grant as more important than the benefits of money-saving collaboration.

Faculty members, too, feel the pull of the federal dollar and suffer the attendant risks. When a position opens for a young professor, a research-oriented department naturally will give preference to someone with a demonstrated ability to attract grant support; this preference may override any questions about the breadth of his or her

---

[19]Dwight D. Eisenhower, "Farewell Radio and Television Address to the American People," January 17, 1961.

scholarship or teaching ability. Even an established faculty member might put aside a promising line of theoretical research to take on a more practical problem backed by plentiful government funds. So the scholar's vaunted mandate to engage in the research he sees as most revealing—the research that will make the greatest contribution to the advancement of science and learning—is undercut. In the competition for scarce resources, both faculty departments and individual professors inevitably feel the pressure to perform the research chores desired by the government.

As a research sponsor, the government naturally avoids abstract problems or those whose answers are interesting only to a small cadre of professional scientists. Government research projects involve practical knowledge and seek quick results. Most professors develop a special affinity for their research material and bring it with them into the classroom. So university students study under the tutelage of research specialists, pondering not the questions that will endure for generations, but practical problems that might be solved—or forgotten—before the students themselves graduate.

Federal support for higher education is a mixed blessing at best. To secure the funds provided by government, universities must become active political lobbyists; to keep the federal dollars flowing, they must satisfy the bureaucracy's insatiable appetite for paperwork. And since the government pays the piper and calls the tunes, universities must tailor their research priorities to match the government's demands. In the end, a heavily subsidized research department can lose all sight of its proper academic goals. Yet the same department can never lose sight of its growing dependence on continued federal support.

Conclusion

The federal government cannot help universities pursue their educational tasks; democratic government is not, and should not be, an appropriate sponsor for liberal arts training. But while it cannot help, the government can certainly hurt. By distracting the universities from their proper role, the federal government has contributed to a serious decline in academic standards and ideals.

Ultimately, the fate of higher education will be decided by the universities themselves. Without a revival of interest in the ultimate goals of liberal education, U.S. universities cannot prosper. The federal government cannot revive that interest, but it can at least stop undermining it.

5

The Courts and Education

by
Thomas R. Ascik

The Supreme Court said in 1960 that "the vigilant protection of constitutional freedoms is nowhere more vital than in the community of American schools."[1] Starting with the cases of *Everson v. Board of Education* (1947) and *Brown v. Board of Education* (1954), and continuing with one precedent-shattering case after another, the Supreme Court has applied the concept of constitutional rights to nearly every aspect of American education. Although the United States recently has been flooded by studies and reports severely critical of the nation's public schools,[2] the historic changes in education wrought by the Supreme Court over the past four decades have hardly been mentioned.

Most critical are those rulings in which the Supreme Court has applied the Constitution to education without prior precedent. These have particularly affected public aid to nonpublic schools, prayer and spiritual values in public schools, racial segregation, and teacher and student rights. In these four areas, the Court, on its own initiative, has broken with the past and established comprehensive national educational policies.

Public Aid to Nonpublic Schools

The authority of any branch of the federal government to intervene in state public policies regarding religion traditionally has been governed by the doctrine of the 1833 case of *Barron v. Baltimore*.[3] In this case, concerning city damage to private property, Chief Justice John Marshall, speaking for a unanimous Supreme Court, ruled that the Court had no jurisdiction over the case because the Bill of Rights

---

[1] *Shelton v. Tucker* 364 U.S. 479 at 487 (1960).
[2] Mortimer Adler, *The Paideia Proposal;* U.S. Department of Education, *A Nation at Risk;* Ernest L. Boyer, *A Report on Secondary Education in America;* Twentieth Century Fund, *Report of the Twentieth Century Fund Task Force on Federal Elementary and Secondary Education Policy,* John Goodlad, *A Place Called School: Prospects for the Future.*
[3] 7 Pet. 243.

placed no restrictions on the actions of city or state governments. The framers of the Bill of Rights had not "intended them to be limitations on the powers of the state governments,"[4] explained Marshall.

In the 1920s and 1930s, however, the Court abandoned *Barron v. Baltimore* and began developing perhaps the most important judicial doctrine of this century: the "incorporation" of the Bill of Rights into the Fourteenth Amendment. That amendment, ratified in 1868, made federal citizenship preeminent over state citizenship and declared in its most important parts that "no state shall . . . . deprive any person of life, liberty, or prosperity, without due process of law; nor deny to any person within its jurisdiction the equal protection of the laws." By incorporating the various rights guaranteed by the Bill of Rights into these Fourteenth Amendment guarantees, the Court gave itself power to overturn state law dealing with almost all areas covered by the ten amendments of the Bill of Rights.

The Court ruled in the 1947 case of *Everson v. Board of Education*,[5] for instance, that the First Amendment's clause prohibiting laws "respecting an establishment of religion" was binding on the states. In this most important Supreme Court education case, except for *Brown v. Board of Education* (1954), the Court was construing the Establishment Clause for the first time. At stake was the constitutionality of a New Jersey statute requiring local school boards to provide free transportation, along established routes, to children attending nonprofit, private (including religiously affiliated) schools.

More significant than the specific ruling in the case was the Court's construction of the First Amendment's Establishment Clause. Declared the Court:

> The "establishment of religion" clause of the First Amendment means at least this: Neither a state nor the Federal Government can set up a church. Neither can it pass laws which aid one religion, aid all religions, or prefer one religion over another. Neither can it force nor influence a person to go to or to remain away from a church against his will or force him to profess a belief or disbelief in any religion. No person can be punished for entertaining or professing religious beliefs or disbeliefs, for church attendance or nonattendance. No tax in any amount, large or small, can be levied to support any religious activities or institutions, whatever they may be called, or whatever form they may adopt to teach or practice religion. Neither a state nor the Federal Government can, openly or secretly, participate in the affairs of any religious organizations or groups and vice versa. In the words of Jefferson, the clause against establishment of religion by law was intended to erect "a wall of

---

[4]This Just Compensation Clause prohibits the federal government from condemning anyone's property without paying him a just compensation for his loss at 249.
[5]330 U.S. 1.

separation between Church and State".... That Amendment requires the state to be neutral in its relations with groups of religious believers and non-believers.[6]

Until this declaration, the most widely held view of the meaning of the Establishment Clause was that it prohibited government preference of one religion over another. When the Supreme Court concluded that states cannot "pass laws which aid one religion, aid all religions, or prefer one religion over another," it introduced for the first time the notion that the Establishment Clause forbade not only government preference of one religion over another but also government preference of religion over nonreligion.

More than 20 years passed before the Court heard its next significant case concerning government aid to religious schools, *Board of Education v. Allen* (1968).[7] In *Allen,* the Court examined a challenge to a New York statute that required local school boards to purchase textbooks (in secular subjects only) and loan them, without charge, to all children enrolled in grades seven through twelve of public or private schools. The books were not limited to those actually in use in the public schools but could include those "designated for use" in the public schools or otherwise approved by the local board of education.

The Court applied *Everson* to the case and decided that the provision of textbooks, like transportation, was a permissible means to the accomplishment of the legitimate state objective of secular education of all children. Religious schools participated in the public interest because "they pursue two goals, religious instruction and secular education."[8] Parochial schools, the Court said, "are performing, in addition to their sectarian function, the task of secular education."[9] This was the birth of the "secular-sectarian" distinction that has defined religious schools as partly serving the public good (the secular subjects in the curriculum) and partly not (religious instruction).

Various cases followed that further defined the principles laid down in *Everson,* including a case dealing with the question of reimbursement to nonpublic schools for their expenditures on teachers of secular subjects and secular institutional materials (*Lemon v. Kurtzman* [1971])[10]. In *Lemon,* the Court ruled the reimbursements unconstitutional because of the danger a teacher under religious control could pose to the separation of the religious from the secular.

---

[6] *Ibid.* at 15-16.
[7] 392 U.S. 236.
[8] *Ibid.* at 243
[9] *Ibid.* at 248.
[10] 403 U.S. 602 (1971)—together with *Early v. DiCenso.*

In *Committee for Public Education and Liberty v. Nyquist* (1973),[11] maintenance and repair grants to nonpublic schools were judged to have the primary effect of advancing religion because the buildings maintained and repaired were not restricted to secular purposes. Also in this case, tuition reimbursements and tuition tax deductions were rejected by the Court as being effectively indistinguishable from aid to the schools themselves: "The effect of the aid is unmistakably to provide desired financial support for nonpublic sectarian institutions."[12] Furthermore, said the Court, states could not "encourage or reward"[13] parents for sending their children to religious schools because this advances religion. Finally, the plan failed the "politically divisive" test because it had the "grave potential" of stimulating "continuing political strife over religion."[14]

Separate strong dissents were filed by Chief Justice Warren Burger and by Justices William Rehnquist and Byron White. Burger thought that there was a definitive difference between government aid to individuals and direct aid to religious institutions. He wrote: "the private individual makes the decision that may indirectly benefit church-sponsored schools; to that extent the state involvement with religion is substantially attenuated."[15] Rehnquist argued that, if the Court could uphold the constitutionality of exempting churches from taxation, then it should similarly uphold the constitutionality of exempting parents from taxation for certain educational expenses. White contended that the Court was ruling as unconstitutional schemes that had "any effect"[16] of advancing religion, whereas the test was properly one of "primary effect."

The Thirty-Years War between the Supreme Court and those states seeking to give public aid to their private schools may have ended with the Supreme Court's 1983 decision in *Mueller v. Allen*.[17] In an opinion written by Justice Rehnquist, a majority of the Court upheld a Minnesota law allowing a deduction on state income taxes for tuition, textbooks, and transportation expenses incurred in the education of students in elementary or secondary schools—public or nonpublic.

Rehnquist decided that the deduction had a secular purpose of "ensuring that the state's citizenry is well-educated"[18] regardless of the type of schools attended. Minnesota also had "a strong public inter-

---

[11]413 U.S. 756.
[12]*Ibid.* at 783.
[13]*Ibid.* at 791.
[14]*Ibid.* at 795.
[15]*Ibid.* at 802.
[16]*Ibid.* at 823.
[17]103 S. Ct. 3062.
[18]*Ibid.* at 3067.

est"[19] in assuring the survival of religious and nonreligious private schools because such schools relieve the public schools of the financial burden of educating a certain percentage of the youth population and because private schools provide "a wholesome competition"[20] for public schools. Furthermore, the primary effect of the law was not the advancement of religion, Rehnquist concluded, in the most important part of his opinion.

Minnesota's plan was distinguished from the tax deductions in *Nyquist* because "the deduction is available for educational expenses incurred by all parents, including those whose children attend public schools and those whose children attend non-sectarian private schools or sectarian private schools."[21] Rehnquist cited the Court's 1981 decision in the *Widmar v. Vincent*[22] ruling that, if a state university makes its facilities available for use by student groups, it must allow student religious groups to use the facilities on an equal basis. In keeping with the *Widmar* decision, Minnesota was here providing benefits on an equal basis to a "broad spectrum of citizens,"[23] and this nondiscriminatory breadth was "an important index of secular effect."[24]

Having thus distinguished *Nyquist,* the Court was then able to say that there is a significant difference, in terms of the Establishment Clause, between providing aid to parents and providing it directly to schools despite the reality that "financial assistance provided to parents ultimately has an economic effect comparable to that of aid given directly to the schools attended by their children."[25] Religious schools received public funds "only as a result of numerous, private choices of individual parents of school-age children,"[26] and this exercise of parental choice caused the financial benefits flowing to religious schools to be much "attentuated."[27]

Implications

The *Mueller* decision and the *Widmar* decision requiring state universities to give "equal access" to student religious groups may signal an emerging Supreme Court view of the relationship of church to state and a possible end to the struggle between the states and the

---

[19]*Ibid.*
[20]*Ibid.,* quoting Justice Powell in *Wolman v. Walter,* 433 U.S. 229 (1977) at 262.
[21]*Ibid.* at 3068.
[22]454 U.S. 263.
[23]*Mueller* at 3069.
[24]*Ibid.* at 3068.
[25]*Ibid.* at 3069.
[26]*Ibid.*
[27]*Ibid.*

Court over public aid for nonpublic education. In *Mueller,* the Court accepted the principle that parents whose children attended religious schools could receive benefits so long as public school parents were equally eligible for benefits. This principle, allowing a state to accommodate its citizens with religious purposes on an equal basis with those pursuing secular purposes, received strong bipartisan support in Congress in 1984. By significant majorities, both Houses passed the "equal access" bill requiring elementary and secondary schools to allow student religious clubs to use their facilities on an equal basis with other student clubs. This was nothing more than the extension of *Widmar* to elementary and secondary schools.

In the U.S., religion has always been the major motivation for the formation and continuation of private schools. Without the *Everson* doctrine, therefore, there would be many more U.S. private schools.

Spiritual Values in Public Schools

The Supreme Court addressed prayer in schools in the 1962 case of *Engle v. Vitale,*[28] a constitutional challenge to the mandated daily recitation of a nondenominational prayer in a New York State school district that said:

Almighty God, we acknowledge our dependence upon Thee, and we beg Thy blessings upon us, our parents, our teachers, and our country.

The prayer had been carefully crafted in consultation with a wide range of Jewish and Christian leaders and officially recommended (in 1951 and 1955) to the state's school districts by the New York State Board of Regents as part of its "Statement on Moral and Spiritual Training in the Schools." In the lower state courts and the New York Court of Appeals (the highest court of New York), the constitutional challenge to the prayer had been rejected with the caveat that no student could be compelled to recite the prayer. Twenty-three other states joined New York in its petition to have the Supreme Court uphold the constitutionality of the prayer. This, however, the Court did not do.

In what might have been unique for such an important case, Justice Hugo Black, writing for the Court, referred to no previous Supreme Court decision as precedent. Instead, he explained the decision by means of an essay on the history of the separation of church and state. Significantly, almost all of the history considered was pre-constitutional—the history of religion in England and the writings of various

[28] 370 U.S. 421.

men, especially Madison and Jefferson, at the time of the ratification of the Constitution and of the Bill of Rights. Justice Potter Stewart, the sole dissenter, argued that the case brought the Free Exercise Clause into consideration in two ways.[29] First, the lack of compulsion meant that the state was not interfering with the free exercise of anyone's religion. Second, the children who wanted to pray were denied the free exercise of their religion, Stewart contended, and they were denied the "opportunity of sharing the spiritual heritage of our Nation."[30] History is relevant, Stewart argued, but not "the history of an established church in sixteenth century England or in eighteenth century America."[31] Instead, the relevant history was the "history of the religious traditions of our people, reflected in countless practices of the institutions and officials of our government."[32]

A year later in the companion cases of *Abington v. Schempp* and *Murray v. Curlett*,[33] the Court struck down state laws requiring the reading of the Bible in public schools. In *Schempp*, the Unitarian plaintiffs challenged a Pennsylvania state law, passed in 1949, requiring the reading of ten verses from the Bible, without comment or interpretation, in the public schools at the beginning of each day. Upon written request, parents could excuse their children from the readings. The plaintiffs had bypassed the Pennsylvania Supreme Court and sued in federal district court, where the law was struck down in a decision based primarily on the *Everson* decision.

In *Murray*, militant atheist Madlyn Murray and her son challenged a 50-year-old rule of the Baltimore School Board requiring the reading of the Lord's Prayer each day in the city's public schools. As in Pennsylvania, parents could excuse their children from the practice. Murray did not request that her son be excused but brought the suit claiming that the rule violated religious liberty by "placing a premium on belief as against non-belief."[34] The Maryland Supreme Court appealed to the U.S. Supreme Court, and eighteen other states joined Maryland's defense of its customs.

The Supreme Court ruled in favor of Murray. *Engle* and especially *Everson* formed the basis of the decision. The Court quoted the *Everson* statement that neither the states nor the federal government "can pass laws which aid one religion, aid all religions, or prefer one religion over another." Once more the Supreme Court was ruling that the influence of religion must be absolutely segregated from the affairs

[29]*Ibid.* at 430.
[30]*Ibid.* at 445.
[31]*Ibid.* at 446.
[32]*Ibid.*
[33]374 U.S. 203.
[34]*Ibid.* at 212.

of state. Finally, the Court invented a test for the establishment of religion: a law is constitutional only if it has "a secular legislative purpose and a primary effect that neither advances nor inhibits religion."[35] According to these principles, the practices in these cases were unconstitutional because they were indisputably exercises of which both purpose and effect were religious. The Court denied that its decision advanced what amounted to a religion of secularism but gave no reason for its denial.

In *Epperson v. Arkansas* (1968),[36] the Supreme Court added a new wrinkle to its judicial attitude toward religion: a law may be unconstitutional, stated the Court, if the legislative motive for passing the law was religious. Since 1928, an Arkansas law prohibited the teaching of evolution in its public schools. The law had never been enforced. In 1965, however, a high school biology teacher, confronted with newly adopted biology textbooks that taught evolution, maintained that she was caught between opposing duties and sued to have the law declared void. In a two-sentence opinion, the Arkansas Supreme Court turned back the challenge by concluding that the law was a "valid exercise of the state's power to specify the curriculum in its public schools."[37]

In addition to the question of religious influence in public schools, at least four other profound issues were involved here: the content of the school curriculum, the authority of states over their public schools, the authority and ability of the federal judiciary to prescribe or proscribe parts of the curriculum, and the growing legal movement to have the federal courts promulgate some First Amendment-based rights of academic freedom. In its resolution of the *Epperson* case, the Supreme Court confined itself to two rationales. The first and more important rationale for the decision was the principle of the *Everson*, *Engle*, and *Schempp* cases. There was no relationship between church and state, the Court said; instead there was a wall. Such a statute clearly violated the "purpose" of the *Schempp* two-part test. The purpose of the statute was clearly religious, and the state did not have the right to make its decisions about school curricula "based upon reasons that violate the First Amendment."[38] In its strongest statement yet about the *Everson* neutrality principle, the Court emphasized that government must treat religion and nonreligion equally, for "the First Amendment mandates government neutrality between religion and religion, and between religion and non-religion."[39]

---

[35]*Ibid.* at 222.
[36]393 U.S. 97.
[37]242 Ark. 922, 416 S.W. 2d 322 (1967).
[38]*Epperson* at 107.
[39]*Ibid.* at 104.

As its second rationale, the Court quoted the statement in *Shelton v. Tucker,* that "the vigilant protection of constitutional freedoms is nowhere more vital than in the community of American schools," and the statement in *Keyishian v. Board of Regents* that the First Amendment will not tolerate "a pall of orthodoxy over the classroom."

Through *Epperson v. Arkansas,* the Court brought the results of constitutional litigation affecting higher education to elementary and secondary schools. To Arkansas' claim that it had constitutional power over its public schools, the Supreme Court declared that the Bill of Rights is applicable everywhere, and constitutional powers are not superior to constitutional rights. Said the Court: "Fundamental values of freedom of speech and inquiry and of belief"[40] are at stake here. Quoting *Keyishian,* "It is much too late to argue that the State may impose upon the teachers in its schools any conditions that it chooses, however restrictive they may be of constitutional guarantees."[41] With this concern for the academic freedom (free speech) of teachers, the Court invented independent rights for teachers to control the curriculum of public schools.

Implications

No court has ever doubted the authority of the states to prescribe moral and spiritual instruction in their public schools. The New York State Board of Regents was exercising that authority when it composed the prayer that became the issue in *Engle.* Today there is a growing consensus that more character training is needed in public schools. Historically, almost all systematic codes of Western morality or developed notions of character have been based on religion.

The effect of these Supreme Court decisions has been to prevent religion from influencing the education of those attending public schools. These decisions have forced those who believe that education cannot be separated from religion and who cannot afford private schools to attend institutions whose governing values are antagonistic to their own. In his concurrence in *Epperson,* Justice Black strongly implied that, if the wall of separation meant that nonreligion may influence the curriculum of public schools but religion may not, then the wall might very well be interfering with the free exercise of religion of some of those in attendance. This is, of course, a step beyond governmental neutrality between religion and nonreligion. Under

---

[40] *Ibid.*
[41] *Ibid.* at 107.

governmental neutrality, the schools are merely indifferent to the values of religious people.

If any statement about the relationship of religion to education is itself a religious statement, then public education that does not discriminate against anyone is impossible under a system of absolute separation of church and state. The only alternative is the opportunity for individuals to exempt themselves at those times when the values presented or implied are antagonistic to their own. But the Court has rejected this principle of voluntariness. So the dilemma grows.

In his dissent in *Schempp,* Justice Stewart said government and religion must necessarily interact. Until *Everson,* they had at least been interacting throughout American history without any of the persecution that the court said it was trying to prevent with the *Engle* decision. In fact, it was *Everson* that launched an unprecedented era of church-state conflict in the U.S., chiefly in the context of education. American history before *Everson* dealt with interaction; since *Everson* it has been the history of conflict. It may be that neutrality is impossible.

Desegregation

An abundance of writing has traced the development of the Supreme Court's doctrine regarding the desegregation of public schools. Three questions place the controversy in perspective: (1) When did the Supreme Court decide that desegegation was incompatible with the American tradition of neighborhood schools? (2) How did the Court come to endorse busing as a remedy for segregation? (3) What has been the attitude of the Court toward education—teaching and learning—in the midst of the desegregation issue?

The fundamental ruling in *Brown v. Board of Education (Brown I),*[42] the most important education case and probably the most important Supreme Court ruling except for *Marbury v. Madison* (1801), was that school systems are forbidden intentionally to segregate the races by law or practice. Yet the Court's basis for this ruling and the full meaning of the ruling have been enigmatic and the cause of much disagreement. Legally, the Court addressed two questions: Does the Constitution forbid segregation; and, if it does, how can the Court get past its own 1896 ruling in *Plessy v. Ferguson*[43] that as long as public policy treated the races "equally," it could require them to be "separate?"

---

[42] 347 U.S. 483.
[43] 163 U.S. 537.

Addressing the "separate but equal" doctrine of *Plessy,* the Court was faced with a situation in which there were "findings . . . . that the Negro and white schools involved have been equalized, or are being equalized, with respect to buildings, curricula, qualifications and salaries of teachers, and other 'tangible' factors."[44] With no deprivation of equality in measurable educational factors, the Court decided to consider whether there was equality of "intangible" factors. It decided that there was not and that the definitive inequality was the separateness itself. The effect on blacks of racial segregation was "a feeling of inferiority as to their status in the community that may affect their hearts and minds in a way unlikely ever to be undone."[45] In its now-famous Footnote Eleven, the Court justified this psychological interpretation and inaugurated a new area of American law by citing the research of various social scientists. "Separate educational facilities are inherently unequal,"[46] the Court concluded. Thus, with this combination of the "separate" with the "equal," the Court effectively overturned *Plessy* in *Brown I* by declaring that modern social science had proved that separate equality was impossible in education.

In reaching this momentous decision, the Court did not address the enormous problem of how to require the dismantling of dual school systems until the following year in the second installment of the same case, *Brown II.*[47] Here, the Court refrained from attempting to declare a universal remedy applicable to every discriminating school system, but concluded, instead, that "because of their proximity to local conditions and the possible need for further hearings, the courts that originally heard those cases can best"[48] fashion specific remedies and, in each case, decide upon the best means to "effectuate a transition to a racially nondiscriminatory school system."[49] This was the beginning of the now commonplace judicial supervision of school systems.

Because the Court in *Brown II* put the burden on school authorities, federal district courts in the South spent the next thirteen years ruling on the constitutionality of various schemes that these authorities fashioned to carry out the mandate of *Brown I.* Only a few cases of significance reached the Supreme Court over this period. In truth, *Brown II* was not much more specific than *Brown I.* Until the Supreme Court's decision in *Green v. New Kent County* (1968), neither the

---

[44]*Brown* at 493.
[45]*Ibid.* at 492.
[46]*Ibid.* at 494.
[47]349 U.S. 294 (1955).
[48]*Ibid.* at 300.
[49]*Ibid.*

lower federal courts nor the school systems knew whether the *Brown* mandate contained a prescription as well as a proscription.

In *Green v. New Kent County*, the Supreme Court announced that it was going to demand more than simply dropping laws requiring segregation. The case concerned the school board of the Virginia county of New Kent, a county with complete racial segregation between its only two schools, which initiated a "freedom-of-choice" plan whereby black and white students could choose which school they wanted to attend. Students not exercising this choice were reassigned to the school they had attended the previous year.

The effect of this plan was to offer to every student, black or white, the opportunity to attend either school, the traditionally all-black school or the traditionally all-white school, while not disturbing the segregated *status quo* if few or no students made the choice. This plan presented the Court with the question whether its *Brown* decision required the changing of the old laws requiring segregation, that is, *de jure* segregation, or the changing of the results of the old laws, that is, *de facto* segregation.

The school board, in effect, was asking the Court to rule on this distinction between *de jure* and *de facto* segregation. In reply, the Court said that it had already done so in *Brown II:* "The Board attempts to cast the issue in its broadest form by arguing that its 'freedom-of-choice' plan may be faulted only by reading the Fourteenth Amendment as universally requiring 'compulsory integration,' a reading it insists the wording of the Amendment will not support. But that argument ignores the thrust of *Brown II*."[50] This "thrust" was the requirement of the "abolition of the system of segregation and its effects,"[51] the Court explained.

The Court here was introducing the notion that segregation had continuing legal effects after the policy of segregation itself was ended. In telling the New Kent School Board that it was not merely freedom or lack of coercion but a certain social result that it was seeking, the Court said that the continuing effects of segregation (what one may have thought was an aspect of *de facto* segregation) were part of *de jure* segregation. In other words, it maintained that it was very unlikely that there could be legally acceptable *de facto* segregation in any district that had a history of *de jure* segregation. A plan was to be measured by its "effectiveness.... in achieving desegregation."[52] Eliminating segregation was not enough; desegregation must be achieved.

---

[50]*Green* at 437.
[51]*Ibid.* at 440.
[52]*Ibid.* at 339.

After *Green,* it was only logical for the Court to endorse busing and racial balance in *Swann v. Charlotte-Mecklenburg Board of Education* (1971).[53] If the prime evidence of the continuing efforts of a defunct policy of segregation was, as the Court said in *Green,* schools that remained heavily one-race, and if a legally enforceable freedom to transfer was ineffective in achieving the redistribution of the two races, then the races must be specifically reassigned to achieve that goal. In *Swann* the Court endorsed three means of reassigning students: racial balances and quotas, busing, and the redrawing of school attendance zones. The Court's rationale for the acceptability of all three was the same: They all worked—that is, they were indisputably "effective" in achieving racial redistribution. *Swann* was the specific application of *Green.*

In summary, the *Brown* decision declared that the problem was that the races were legally required to be separate—not the inequality of facilities, curricula, or staff between black and white schools. The Court ruled that separation was itself an inequality (a psychological inequality) and was unconstitutional. In *Green,* the Court found that the continuing effect of segregation was the continuing separation of the races, and this finding was used to justify race-conscious student reassignment in *Swann.*

In *Milliken v. Bradley* (1977) (*Milliken II*),[54] however, the Court concluded what, on its face, seemed to be a contradiction not only of *Green* but also of *Brown.* The main issue of the case was "the question whether federal courts can order remedial education programs as part of a school desegregation decree."[55]

In *Milliken II,* the defendant Detroit school system charged that the district court's remedy of requiring the system to undertake the retraining of teachers and provide remedial reading and testing and counseling services to black children was not based on the nature of the constitutional violation; and that "the Court's decree must be limited to remedying unlawful pupil assignments."[56] In rejecting this argument, the Court answered that a federal court's power to fashion remedies was "broad and flexible."[57]

What the Court really did in *Milliken II* was extend the "continuing effects" of *Green* while doing away with the "separation" basis for *Brown* and *Green.* "Discriminatory student assignment policies can themselves manifest and breed other inequalities built into a dual

---
[53] 402 U.S. 1.
[54] 433 U.S. 267.
[55] *Ibid.* at 279.
[56] *Ibid.* at 270.
[57] *Ibid.* at 281.

system based on racial discrimination..... Pupil assignment also does not automatically remedy the impact of previous, unlawful educational isolation,"[58] the Court concluded. For the first time, the Court was saying that there was a justifiable "impact" of racial separation beyond the separation itself.

Implications

In many cities where the question of busing has become moot because blacks have come to comprise the majority of the enrollment, the courts are more interested today in educational remedies than in busing and other remedies of mandatory student reassignment. This often becomes quite detailed, with the judge prescribing not only specific remedial programs but also the books to be used in such programs. Thus judges have taken over educational duties.

The *Brown* decision, the Civil Rights Act of 1964, the Voting Rights Act, and other laws have helped to change black political impotence to power. The full participation of blacks in government policy making may allow judges to permit the revival of local control of schools. If the courts are convinced that there are no impediments to black equality of political opportunity, they may be willing to give back control of the schools to communities, parents, and educators. This would allow the courts to avoid the problem of judicial prescription of the school curriculum. And it may be a necessity for the educational and social welfare of the children.

Contemporary research in education suggests that community and parent involvement and a shared sense of purpose are central to an effective school.[59] A federal district court recently endorsed these conclusions in the desegregation case involving the school system of Norfolk, Virginia. Faced with the obvious failure of busing,[60] the

---

[58]*Ibid.* at 283, 287-88.

[59]See: Thomas Ascik, "Looking at Some Research on What Makes An Effective School" in *Blueprint for Educational Reform,* The Free Congress Foundation, Summer 1984. Also, inter alia: Richard Murnane, "Interpreting the Evidence on School Effectiveness," *Teachers College Record,* Fall 1981; Thomas Corcoran and Barbara Hansen, "The Quest for Excellence: Making Public Schools More Effective," The New Jersey School Boards Association, 1983; Gilbert Austin, "Exemplary Schools and the Search for Effectiveness," *Educational Leadership,* October 1979; and Edgar Epps, "Towards Effective Desegregated Schools," paper commissioned by the National Institute of Education, 1983.

[60]David Armor, "The Evidence on Busing," *The Public Interest,* 28, 1972; and James Coleman, "Recent Trends in School Integration," *Educational Researcher,* July-August 1975; Dennis Cuddy, "The Problem of Forced Busing and a Possible Solution," *Phi Delta Kappan,* September 1984.

dubious status of the "self-image" social psychology incorporated into *Brown*,[61] and the difficulties of judicial supervision of the curriculum, the courts may have to turn to other means to guarantee equality of educational opportunity for all children.

The Rights of Teachers and Students

The first important case applying the constitutional principle of free speech to the field of education was *Shelton v. Tucker* (1960).[62] One of the most important First Amendment cases, it was decided by a narrow 5 to 4 margin. An Arkansas statute required prospective teachers at public schools or colleges to disclose every organization to which he or she had belonged or contributed regularly in the preceding five years. Some teachers who refused to do so, challenged the statute as a deprivation of their "rights to personal association, and academic liberty, protected by the Due Process Clause of the Fourteenth Amendment from invasion by state action."[63]

In overruling the Arkansas Supreme Court, which had upheld the statute, the Supreme Court said that this case differed from that group of First Amendment cases[64] in which the Court had invalidated state statutes because the statutes did not really serve a legitimate governmental purpose. Here, there was "no question of the relevance of a State's inquiry into the fitness and competence of its teachers."[65] Nevertheless, without any discussion at all, the Court immediately reached two definitive conclusions.

1) It declared that teachers had "a right of free association, a right closely allied to freedom of speech and a right which, like free speech, lies at the foundation of a free society."[66]

2) Rather than consider the issue of the permissible qualifications that a state may place on public employment, or the question of the uniqueness of teachers as public employees, the Court asserted that a constitutionally protected "personal freedom"[67] of teachers was at stake here. At stake were "freedom of speech . . . . freedom of in-

---

[61]"School Desegregation, The Social Science Role," *American Psychologist*, 38, 8, August 1983; Walter G. Stephan, "Blacks and Brown: The Effects of School Desegregation on Black Students," *School Desegregation and Black Achievement*, National Institute of Education, 1984.
[62]364 U.S. 484.
[63]*Ibid.* at 485.
[64]E.g. *NAACP v. Alabama*, 357 U.S. 449 (1958).
[65]*Shelton* at 485.
[66]*Ibid.* at 486.
[67]*Ibid.*

quiry.... freedom of association.... the free spirit of teachers.... the free play of the spirit.... the free[dom] to inquire, to study and to evaluate."[68] Consequently, "the vigilant protection of constitutional freedoms is nowhere more vital than in the community of American schools."[69] This last statement and the two conclusions upon which it is based have presaged most of the substance of other key cases.

The Court found that a teacher could have many associations that would have no bearing upon the teacher's competence or fitness. Therefore, "The statute's comprehensive interference with associational freedom goes far beyond what might be justified in the exercise of the State's legitimate inquiry into the fitness and competency of its teachers."[70] The four dissenters all joined two separate dissents written by Justices John Harlan and Felix Frankfurter. Their similar arguments had two main points. First, there was no evidence that the information collected had ever been abused or used in a discriminatory manner. Secondly, this was a reasonable and not excessive way for the state to exercise its conceded right to inquire into the fitness of its teachers.

That a major change had been effected in the attitude of the federal judiciary to the situation of teachers in government-operated schools was made evident in *Keyishian v. Board of Regents of New York* (1967).[71] In *Keyishian,* the Court overturned the same New York "loyalty oath" law that it had sustained fifteen years earlier in *Adler v. Board of Education.*[72] The law excluded anyone from public employment who advocated the overthrow of the government by force or violence. Pursuant to the law, the Board of Regents of the state university system had required university employees to certify that they were not members of the Communist Party or, if they were, that they had communicated the fact to the president of the university. Keyishian and three other faculty members refused to certify themselves and challenged the constitutionality of the law and its application.

In *Adler,* the Court had turned back such a challenge and declared:

> A teacher works in a sensitive area in a classroom. There he shapes the attitude of young minds toward the society in which they live. In this, the state has a vital concern. It must preserve the integrity of the schools. That the school authorities have the right and the duty to screen the officials, teachers, and employees as to their fitness to maintain the integrity of the schools as a part of ordered society, cannot be doubted.[73]

---

[68]*Ibid.* at 487.
[69]*Ibid.*
[70]*Ibid.* at 490.
[71]385 U.S. 589.
[72] 342 U.S. 485
[73]*Ibid.* at 493.

But in *Keyishian,* the Court decided that the New York law was unconstitutional. Declared the Court:

> There can be no doubt of the legitimacy of New York's interest in protecting its education system from subversion. But "even though the governmental purpose be legitimate and substantial, that purpose cannot be pursued by means that broadly stifle fundamental personal liberties when the end can be more narrowly achieved." *Shelton v. Tucker.* . . . "The vigilant protection of constitutional freedoms is nowhere more vital than in the community of American schools." *Shelton v. Tucker.*[74]

In *Adler,* the Court had said that teachers "may work for the school system upon the reasonable terms laid down by the proper authorities of New York. If they do not choose to work on such terms, they are at liberty to retain their beliefs and association and go elsewhere."[75] But throughout the *Keyishian* opinion, the Court cited numerous cases that it had decided in the area of the First Amendment since 1952. What had happened between 1952 and 1967 was that the reach of the First Amendment had been dramatically extended by the Court.

In the 1968 case of *Pickering v. Board of Education,*[76] the *Shelton* and *Keyishian* rationales for freedom of association for teachers were applied by the Supreme Court to freedom of speech for teachers. A county board of education in Illinois had dismissed a teacher, after a public hearing, for publishing a letter in a newspaper criticizing the board's performance in the area of school finance. The board found that numerous statements in the letter were false and that the publication of the statements unjustifiably impugned the board and the school administration.

The Supreme Court found that the teacher's right to free speech prevented his dismissal:

> To the extent that the Illinois Supreme Court's opinion may be read to suggest that teachers may constitutionally be compelled to relinquish the First Amendment rights they would otherwise enjoy as citizens to comment on matters of public interest in connection with the operation of the public schools in which they work, it proceeds on a premise that has been unequivocally rejected in numerous prior decisions of this Court. . . . *Shelton v. Tucker.* . . . *Keyishian v. Board of Regents.* . . . "The theory that public employment which may be denied altogether may be subjected to any conditions, regardless of how unreasonable, has been uniformly rejected." *Keyishian v. Board of Regents.* . . . the threat of dismissal from public employment is nonetheless a potent means of inhibiting speech.[77]

---

[74]*Keyishian* at 602-03.
[75]*Adler* at 492.
[76]*Keyishian* at 605-06.
[77]391 U.S. 563.

In *Tinker v. Des Moines* (1969),[78] the rights established in *Shelton* and *Keyishian* were extended to students:

> First Amendment rights, applied in light of the special characteristics of the school environment, are available to teachers and students. It can hardly be argued that either students or teachers shed their constitutional rights to freedom of speech or expression at the schoolhouse gate.[79]

The case stemmed from the deliberate defiance of a school system's rule prohibiting the wearing of armbands—in this instance protesting the Vietnam War. "Our problem," the Court said, "lies in the area where students in the exercise of First Amendment rights collide with the rules of the school authorities."[80] Wearing of armbands was akin to "pure speech" and implicated "direct, primary First Amendment rights."[81] The students' expression of their political views by wearing armbands had caused no disorder or disturbance in the schools, had not interfered with the schools' work, and had not intruded upon the rights of other students. Furthermore, the mere fear of a disturbance was not reason enough to justify this curtailment of speech, the Court decided, because "our Constitution says we must take this risk."[82] With this ruling, the Court established a new presumption in American education. "In the absence of a specific showing of constitutionally valid reasons to regulate their speech, students are entitled to freedom of expression of their views."[83]

In a scorching dissent, Justice Black, a lifelong First Amendment advocate, asserted that the Court had launched a "new revolutionary era of permissiveness in this country fostered by the judiciary"[84] by arrogating to itself "rather than to the State's elected officials charged with running the schools, the decision as to which school disciplinary regulations are 'reasonable.'"[85] Although he did not explicitly deny that students have free speech rights, Black may have argued so in effect, writing: "Nor are public school students sent to the schools at public expense to broadcast political or any other views to educate and inform the public ... taxpayers send children to school on the premise that at their age they need to learn, not teach."[86]

With its decision, the Court reversed what had been the unquestioned social agreement that school authorities were to be obeyed

---

[78]*Ibid.* at 568, 574.
[79]393 U.S. 503.
[80]*Ibid.* at 506.
[81]*Ibid.* at 507.
[82]*Ibid.* at 508.
[83]*Ibid.* at 509.
[84]*Ibid.* at 511.
[85]*Ibid.* at 518.
[86]*Ibid.* at 517.

always and that only in the rarest and most extraordinary cases, where a student had been seriously wronged, could a redress of grievances be pursued. Now, with regard to speech in schools, the reasons for student obedience must be demonstrable beforehand.

Implications

The issue of the *Brown* case was student assignment; in *Everson* and its progeny, the Supreme Court was intervening to prevent religion from influencing education. In both areas, the Court rearranged traditional ways of doing things in American education. However, when it applied the constitutional principles of freedom of speech and freedom of association to education, the Court added to the educational enterprise. To the business of teaching and learning were added "direct, primary First Amendment rights" of teachers and students, that is to say, personal liberties, independent of educational purposes but applied to education, enforceable in a court of law.

Schools have a purpose other than that for which they were established, the Supreme Court has said. This purpose is often called "academic freedom," and as the Supreme Court has outlined, it is protected by courts even when not desired by those who founded, and continue to fund, the public schools. For students, it means that they have a legally enforceable right to do other things than learn at school. And for teachers, it means that they have a legally enforceable right to be employed at schools, regardless of whether the school authorities want them there, and a legally enforceable right to say things other than what the school hired them to say. These rights, especially with the powerful presumptions that they carry with them, have fundamentally altered the school board-teacher and teacher-student relationships.

6

A New Agenda for Education

The recurring theme of this volume is that centralized control of education has failed.

Teacher training has fallen under the control of university departments of education and education accreditation agencies that perpetuate questionable social ideologies and shun high standards. Teachers' unions (most notably, the NEA) have stripped administrators of power, opposed plans to share responsibility for education with parents, sought to control the curriculum without collaboration with those whose children they are educating, and demanded more money while rejecting accountability. What is worse, these unions support political candidates who agree to advance their interests.

Centralized control of elementary and secondary education has redirected local and state education priorities into subsidiary agendas. It has skewed balanced education programs and crowded out the core competencies. Control has been taken from the people and placed in the hands of small but powerful lobbies motivated by flawed premises. Special interest programs based on these flawed premises are then advanced. The inevitable result has been the sacrifice of educational excellence and integrity.

American universities have allowed traditional academic ideals to be undermined by accepting the federal agendas (such as affirmative action) that accompany federal money. As a result, political goals have usurped those of higher education, and the very purpose of the university has been altered dramatically—to the detriment of quality teaching and academic standards.

To make matters worse, the Supreme Court has applied the Constitution to education without prior precedent. So doing, it has established a comprehensive national policy in several critical areas, including public aid to nonpublic schools, prayer and spiritual values, racial segregation, and student rights. Court decisions have reinterpreted the Establishment Clause, triggering endless conflicts over church/state affairs; usurped states' rights to prescribe moral and spiritual instruction in their public schools, opening the classroom doors to "values-free" education; established judicial supervision of desegregation, creating white flight and the resegregation of the schools; and arrogated to the judiciary the right to set local school disciplinary standards, thereby crippling the power of school authorities to effect discipline in their own schools. Caught in its own tangled web, the Court is only now seeking ways to free itself and the nation from these counterproductive decisions.

Major changes are needed to reverse the damage from the hammerlock of centralized control on education. The following specific actions should help place U.S. schooling once again on sound, independent footing, where it works best.

The Teaching Profession

1. Separate departments of education in the nation's schools and colleges should be eliminated or reformed. Pedagogical instruction should be transferred to departments of academic instruction.

2. Aspiring teachers should pass an examination testing their mastery of academic disciplines and aptitude for teaching.

3. Every novice teacher should serve a year's apprenticeship under competent supervision.

4. Outstanding teachers should be recognized formally and rewarded as Master Teachers, which would make them exemplars for others and supervisors of apprentice teachers.

5. Advancement of teachers via "career ladders" and merit pay should be determined by teaching success, not by accumulation of seniority and education credits.

6. To retain certification, teachers should be retested after fixed periods on the job, with successive examinations progressively more exacting.

Public and Private Schools

1. Passage of tuition tax credit and voucher legislation at the federal and/or state levels should be a top legislative priority.

2. Legislation specifically should state that those institutions benefitting from tuition tax credits or vouchers are not to be deemed recipients of federal aid or subsidies.

3. As long as a religion is not being established by the state, public aid to religious schools should not be considered unconstitutional.

The Growth of the Federal Role in Education

1. The President should encourage a national debate on the merits of centralized vis-à-vis decentralized education. He should appoint a

national commission to hold hearings across the country, review the ample evidence, and publish a report.

2. The Commission should study and make recommendations on what constitutes a proper education for handicapped children and who has the primary responsibility for this education.

3. Chapter 1 of the 1981 Omnibus Budget Reconciliation Act should be reconstituted as a voucher program, as the Reagan Administration has proposed, or folded into a block grant and turned over to the states. Chapter 1 has failed to accomplish its aim of significantly and permanently raising the academic achievement of low-income, slow students. The costs are excessively disproportionate to its benefits, and it has created a new deprived group—the high achievers. The way to help educationally deprived, low-income students is to give parents real discretion (through vouchers) in choosing the schools their children attend or (through block grants) to spend the money locally to meet the unique needs of each school district.

4. The U.S. must confirm English unequivocally as the nation's one and only official language. To support bilingual education is to encourage fragmentation. All students who attend U.S. schools should be taught—from the beginning—in English.

5. The Women's Educational Equity Act has advanced a radical feminist agenda in our public schools. It should be repealed.

Higher Education

1. Through legislation, Congress should narrow the federal government's authority to intervene in academic affairs. Federal guidelines and the accompanying paperwork should apply only to those schools that accept direct federal support. The federal government should retain its authority to prosecute an institution violating federal antidiscrimination statutes. A school that does not accept direct federal support, however, should not be subject to federal regulations merely because its student body includes some recipients of government loans. Congress should end the uncertainty and make this point clear.

2. Affirmative action programs must be revamped, so that government efforts to prevent illegal discrimination do not burden nonliable institutions with onerous paperwork. Unless there is evidence of illegal discrimination, Washington should not interfere in the academic affairs of an institution. Federal agencies should not set quotas for the admission of students or the appointment of faculty members.

3. When Washington's research needs can be met by university resources (though nonacademic research institutions may be equally capable of filling those needs), the appropriate federal agency should

enter a contractual relationship with the school involved. Federal research grants do not justify Washington's involvement in the school's general academic affairs. Nor should the U.S. Department of Education be involved in what should be a simple contractual relationship between a university and another arm of the federal government.

The Courts and Education

1. The Supreme Court's 1983 decision in *Mueller v. Allen* established the legality of the Minnesota law allowing parents of public and nonpublic school children to deduct tuition and additional education expenses from their income taxes. Other states should take advantage of this ruling and adopt a similar or identical program.

2. The *Everson* Supreme Court decision of 1947, which reinterpreted the Establishment Clause to mandate an "absolute wall of separation between church and state" has little basis in constitutional law or tradition. On this, most constitutional scholars agree.[1] The ruling has produced more conflicts than it has resolutions of church/state interactions. The Constitution clearly contemplates local resolution of this issue. Therefore, the Court should take the first opportunity to overturn the *Everson* decision, as it has overturned others.

3. There needs to be a national desegregation remedy other than forced busing, which would place the power of decision in the hands of the minorities involved. Such national voluntary school integration recently has been proposed by Dennis Cuddy, a senior associate with the National Institute of Education. Dr. Cuddy argues that forced busing to achieve racial balance discriminates against the minority race, because it is bused in greater proportion to the majority race. Forced busing, therefore, should be prohibited, and no one should be denied the right to attend his or her neighborhood school. To avoid coercive resegregation, Dr. Cuddy proposes that any student receive free transportation to attend any school within the district if the court rules that racial discrimination in educational opportunities exists in his or her home school.[2]

4. There needs to be a national discussion about the impact of the Supreme Court decisions—most notably *Tinker v. Des Moines* which

---

[1] Peter J. Ferrara, *Religion and the Constitution: A Reinterpretation* (Washington, D.C.: Free Congress Research & Education Foundation, 1983).

[2] Dennis L. Cuddy, "The Problems of Forced Busing and a Possible Solution," *Phi Delta Kappan,* September 1984, pp. 55-56.

extended First Amendment rights to students—that have replaced the traditional student/teacher relationship with an adversarial, legal model and have usurped the right of state and local education officials to set their own disciplinary standards. This appears to have damaged the teacher/student relationship. The Supreme Court is not always aware of the long-run social effects of its rulings. A Commission should be established, therefore, as a focal point for discussion and a source of recommendations to the Court.

* * * * * *

The reversal of most of these flawed policies could be effected over the next four years of the Reagan Administration. Such measures are compatible with many other goals of the Reagan mandate, in which the people have indicated their desire to return social policy to the local and state levels. Given such impetus, it seems clear that the time for a new agenda is now.

Contributors

Thomas R. Ascik, a lawyer and former teacher, is a Senior Research Associate in the Law and Public Management Division of the National Institute of Education, U.S. Department of Education.

Eileen M. Gardner, a former teacher, is the M. J. Murdock Fellow in Education Policy Studies at The Heritage Foundation.

Annette Kirk (Mrs. Russell Kirk) was a very active member of the Naitonal Commission on Excellence in Education. She has been a school-board member, and is the mother of four daughters at various levels of schooling—some in public schools, some in independent schools.

Dr. Russell Kirk is the director of the social-science program of the Educational Research Council of America, editor of *The University Bookman*, and author of *Decadence and Renewal in the Higher Learning, Academic Freedom, The Intemperate Professor, St. Andrews,* and other books.

Philip F. Lawler, the President of the American Catholic Conference, was formerly Director of Studies at The Heritage Foundation. He is the author of *Coughing in Ink: The Demise of Academic Ideals.*

K. Alan Snyder was formerly Headmaster of Berean Christian Academy in Chesapeake, Virginia, and is now the Director of the Historical-Political Research Services in Fairfax Station, Virginia.